P9-DWT-258

Essays and Studies 1991

The English Association

The object of the English Association is to promote the knowledge and appreciation of English language and literature.

The Association pursues these aims by creating opportunities of co-operation among all those interested in English; by furthering the recognition of English as essential in education; by discussing methods of English teaching; by holding lectures, conferences, and other meetings; by publishing a journal, books, and leaflets; and by forming local branches overseas and at home.

Publications

The Year's Work in English Studies. An annual bibliography. Published by Blackwell (U.S.A.: Humanities Press).

Essays and Studies. An annual volume of essays by various scholars assembled by the collector covering usually a wide range of subjects and authors from the medieval to the modern. Published by D.S. Brewer.

English. The journal of the Association, *English* is published three times a year by the Association.

Newsletter. A *Newsletter* is published three times a year giving information about forthcoming publications, conferences, and other matters of interest.

Benefits of Membership

Institutional Membership

Full members receive copies of *The Year's Work in English Studies*, *Essays and Studies*, *English* (3 issues) and three *Newsletters*.

Ordinary Membership covers *English* (3 issues) and three *Newsletters*.

Schools Membership includes two copies of each issue of *English*, one copy of *Essays and Studies*, three *Newsletters*, and preferential booking and rates for various conferences held by the Association.

Individual Membership

Individuals take out Basic Membership, which entitles them to buy all regular publications of the English Association at a discounted price, and attend Association gatherings.

For further details write to The Secretary, The English Association,
The Vicarage, Priory Gardens, London W4 1TT.

Essays and Studies 1991

History and the Novel

Edited by
Angus Easson

for the English Association

D.S. BREWER

ESSAYS AND STUDIES 1991
IS VOLUME FORTY-FOUR IN THE NEW SERIES
OF ESSAYS AND STUDIES COLLECTED ON BEHALF OF
THE ENGLISH ASSOCIATION
ISSN 0071-1357

© The English Association 1991

All Rights Reserved
Unauthorised duplication contravenes applicable laws

First published 1991 by D.S. Brewer, Cambridge

D.S. Brewer is an imprint of Boydell & Brewer Ltd
PO Box 9, Woodbridge, Suffolk IP12 3DF
and of Boydell & Brewer Inc.
PO Box 41026, Rochester, NY 14604, USA

ISBN 0 85991 322 8

British Library Cataloguing-in-Publication Data
Easson, Angus
Essays and studies: 1991: History and the novel.
– (English Association: essays and studies)
I. Title II. Series
809.3
ISBN 0-85991-322-8

The Library of Congress has cataloged this serial publication:
Catalog card number 36-8431

This publication is printed on acid-free paper

Printed in Great Britain by
St Edmundsbury Press Ltd, Bury St Edmunds, Suffolk

Contents

PR 13 E58 1991
Essays and studies
v. 44
University of the Pacific
Library
Received on: 08-07-91

Painting and the Past

LEONEE ORMOND

Fiction and history are kindred forms. Indeed, as late as the eighteenth century, history was regarded as a literary art. Both fiction and history are narrative structures, concerned with the behaviour of human beings and with the passage of time. Modern historians, wary of using fiction as source material, stress the scientific accuracy of their own discipline, although choice and discrimination work to produce an individual construct, not a set of statistics. Fiction, on its side, has a strongly historical dimension. Even aggressively contemporary works frequently turn their attention to the past, if only in stating or implying a contrast.

This essay is concerned with some of the ways in which reference to paintings (whether known or invented) introduces an historical dimension into fiction. Paintings, like sculptures or archaeological finds, have the timelessness of the solid object. They come down from the past in a concrete form, whereas music and literature are continuously reinterpreted through time.

Paintings, however, are not innocent objects or mere conveyers of a tangible past. They reflect the culture and stylistic conventions of the period which produced them, and their survival and familiarity depend upon the attitudes of later generations. A novelist who chooses to refer to an old master painting is making (however loosely) a connection between past and present. A painting does not, of course, actually appear in a novel as a tangible object. Whether loosely mentioned, or fully described, it must lose its solid quality, be textualized, existing as language, not paint and canvas.

It is important, at the outset, to distinguish between different kinds of fictional reference to painting. In an historical novel, the function of such reference is to convey the authenticity of the narrative. When Thackeray tells us that Barry Lyndon and his family sat to Sir Joshua Reynolds, and were painted as Hector, Andromache, and Astyanax, he is making sure that he gets the right painter for the period, and the right kind of subject for that painter. Reynolds specialised in posing his sitters in classical guise, as in *The Duchess of Manchester and her son, Lord Mandeville, in the character of Diana disarming Love* of 1769 (National Trust, Wimpole Hall). Thackeray is also pointing up the absurdity of the pose, particularly for the upstart speaker: 'I was represented as quitting my wife, in the costume of the Tippleton yeomanry, of which I was major: the child starting back from my helmet' (ch. 17).[1]

Another kind of reference belongs to the narrative itself, where the work of art is seen by the characters as an historical object within the inner and contemporary world of the novel. In Virginia Woolf's *Night and Day*, Katharine Hilbery, attempting to square Victorianism, in which her family are rooted, with the early twentieth-century world in which she lives, finds the forces of her upbringing represented in the iconic portrait of her grandfather, Richard Alardyce, a poet in the Tennyson mould. The same point is made when the narrator explains that the family telephone, a modern touch in a novel of 1919, is surrounded by prints 'of great-uncles, famed for their prowess in the East'. In the middle of a telephone conversation with a young man from a different background to her own, Katherine

> looked fixedly at the print of the great-uncle who had not ceased to gaze, with an air of amiable authority, into a world which, as yet, beheld no symptoms of the Indian Mutiny. And yet, gently swinging against the wall, within the black tube, was a voice which recked nothing of Uncle James. (ch. 24)

A third kind of reference is metaphorical rather than actual, and can belong to the narrator as well as to the characters. In Ruth Prawer Jhabvala's *Heat and Dust* (1975), Harry, an Englishman, describing Olivia's escape from disgrace in the British compound, is reminded of a print, *Mrs. Secombe in Flight from the Mutineers*: 'Mrs. Secombe was also in native dress and in a state of great agitation, with her hair awry and smears of dirt on her face'. The vignette recalls the hardening of British attitudes to Indians in the aftermath of the mutiny. It is against this climate of opinion that Olivia has transgressed in her affair with the Nawab. Like the passage from *Barry Lyndon*, this vivid and economical account has a touch of absurdity: 'Olivia was also in flight – but, as Harry pointed out, in the opposite direction' (p. 172).

These distinctions between different kinds of reference are intended to provide an introduction rather than an overall framework for a discussion of particular examples. They are, in any case, neither exclusive nor complete. The first (purely historical) definition can

1 References, in the text, are to chapters where the novels are conveniently divided, or to pages of the edition of which the date is given.

always include the second (the encounter), and the third (the metaphor) can occur at any time. I will, however, open with two examples taken from my first category, before looking at some of those encounters between characters and paintings which belong to my second group. The emphasis in this section will fall first upon the discussion of portraiture and then on the use of the 'gallery episode' in later nineteenth-century fiction. Some examples of metaphoric reference will be considered in this final part.

My two historical fictions, George Eliot's *Romola* and Violet Needham's *The Boy in Red*, are not as straightforward as they seem. In *Romola*, Eliot introduces a real Florentine painter, Piero di Cosimo, as a character, and makes him paint fictional pictures, the subject-matter of which plays a part in our understanding of the characters. Only one painting mentioned in the novel, *Venus, Cupid, and Mars*, is a known work by Piero. *Romola* clearly belongs to my first group, introducing old master paintings as part of an elaborate historical recreation. Yet, within *Romola*, there is more than one historical level. In Savonarola's convent, San Marco, are frescoes by Fra Angelico, historical objects in Savonarola's time, as they were in George Eliot's. She herself, as a woman, never saw them, and had to rely upon G. H. Lewes's description for her account of Tito Melema's glimpse in chapter 64. Here, the purity of the image contrasts with both Tito's perfidy and with Savonarola's tension and intensity, recalling an age of simple religious faith, now lost forever.

George Eliot was stimulated by the wealth of painting to be found in Florence. She was not alone; an interest in the Italian old masters spread rapidly as travel became easier and new galleries were opened in Northern Europe. George Eliot, like Robert Browning, drew upon reference-works like Giorgio Vasari's *Lives of the Painters*, and she scatters *Romola* with precise details of works in Florence. Of Bernardo Dovizi, for example, we are told that he 'now looks at us out of Raphael's portrait as the keen-eyed Cardinal da Bibbiena' (ch. 20; Pitti Palace, Florence). Dovizi's character is revealed to us through his image as an older man. Similarly, in the account of a *Virgin and Child* in the convent of San Marco, we are told that it is the work of 'that young painter' who had still to take his vows and change his name to Fra Bartolommeo (ch. 49).

The historical setting of *Romola*, and its treatment of Florentine political life, has been related to British interest in the Italian risorgimento. For a later piece of historical writing, *The Boy in Red*, published for an audience of young people in 1945, Violet Needham chose the age of William the Silent, the sixteenth-century saviour of the Netherlands. The subject had a contemporary association, and the Spanish invaders can be paralleled with the Nazis, whose occupation of Holland ended in 1945. In praising the courage and ingenuity of the sixteenth-century Dutch, Needham opens up a parallel with her own day.

Fiction, history, and the fine arts are rarely as closely associated as they are in Needham's 'Prologue' to *The Boy in Red*, where the narrator tells of an early acquaintance with a particular painting:

> It portrayed a boy of some twelve or fourteen years of age in a scarlet tunic and cap and a falcon on his wrist; not a pretty child, but one of confident bearing, and the single pheasant's feather in his scarlet cap gave him in some unaccountable fashion a gallant and attractive air. His figure stood out in bold relief against a dark background with other children to whom the boy appeared to pay little attention and perhaps for that reason I did not either, my interest was centred on the boy in red. (p. 13)

This is an *ecphrasis*, a detailed description of a painting, and it juxtaposes two periods of time, that of the painting's own age and that of the moment of observation. Here, the narrator's observation has inspired a work of historical fiction, in which the boy from the painting plays a leading rôle. The association proposed is an intriguing empathy. The narrator in childhood has been attracted by the portrait of another child, and through that early attraction a whole area of history has been revealed. Needham's method here is a comparatively complex one. The portrait (which may or may not be based upon an actual work of art) is a fictional artefact encapsulating certain preoccupations about seventeenth-century Holland. The boy is 'gallant', 'confident', and independent, he stands apart from the other children, as Holland stood almost alone in her opposition to Spain. As a framed object, the portrait represents a direct link with the historical past, a frozen image which then 'unfreezes' to open up the narrative. In Needham's 'Prologue' there are two levels of past childhood, that of the distant and that of the more recent past. The children are fixed in memory, one in the painting, the other, now an adult, looking back.

The introduction of portraiture is by far the most frequently used and the most straightforward way of referring to history through painting. It also supplies the clearest instances of my second category, the encounter between the fictional character and the work of art.

Dickens, with his keen sense of the disparity between the projected image and the reality, was irritated by the hypocrisy of public portraiture. In two novels of his middle period, *Dombey and Son* and *Bleak House*, he uses the concept of the family picture gallery to encapsulate certain radical observations about royalty, the aristocracy, and their part in history. In both cases, there is a strong satirical impulse. Mr Dombey, as Dickens himself had done in 1838, tours Warwick castle in the company of Mrs Skewton and her daughter, Edith, whom he is to marry. The pictures on the wall provide a commentary on this misalliance. The two lions (then attributed to Rubens and still in Warwick Castle) are 'animals, opposed by nature', who worry each other. The Rubens painting of St Ignatius Loyola is presumably the original of the 'churchman, with his hand upraised', who denounces 'the mockery of such a couple coming to God's altar' (ch. 27; Norton Simon Foundation).

Even more telling is the passage where Mrs Skewton apostrophises two Tudor portraits: one the Coronation painting of Queen Elizabeth (National Portrait Gallery) and the other a version of the Holbein *Henry VIII* (Warwick Castle), as respectively 'that inestimable Queen Bess' and 'such a picture . . . with his dear little peepy eyes, and his benevolent chin!' (ch. 27). Dickens's general distaste for the idealising of the historical past sharpens the satire here. He regarded Elizabeth I as unwomanly and, in his view, Mrs Skewton has much in common with her, both being women who refuse to accept the advance of age. Mention of the much-married Henry VIII gives the reader notice that Mr Dombey is about to be disappointed again. He too wants only sons, regarding women as no more than a means to an end.

This passage displays Dickens's historical sense, but it is most effective as an account of the modern world of the novel. The weight of the historical past is felt more keenly in *Bleak House*, where the novelist uses the Dedlock family portraits at Chesney Wold as a metaphor for the dead hand of paternalism and patronage. Members of the Dedlock family have been painted as great commanders or admirals, as chaste virgin saints or as simpering pastoral maidens with hayrakes. In this artificial guise, they have presented themselves to posterity, and posterity, for want of any other evidence, is forced to accept these frozen and untruthful images of the past. For Sir Leicester Dedlock, and others like him, this lineage represents an ultimate sanction for conservatism, a conservatism which tolerates the legal case of Jarndyce and Jarndyce or the slum of Tom All Alone's. Dickens's introduction of the Dedlock portraits, on more than one occasion in the novel, underlines his point emphatically.

Dickens's practice in using family portraits as a shorthand for tradition is echoed by other nineteenth-century novelists. Thackeray, for example, makes a similar and frequent use of portraiture. In *The Newcomes*, a visit to a country house is expressed in a single sentence:

> The housekeeper, pattering on before us from chamber to chamber, was expatiating upon the magnificence of this picture; the beauty of that statue; the marvellous richness of those hangings and carpets; the admirable likeness of the late Marquis by Sir Thomas; of his father, the fifth Earl, by Sir Joshua, and so on. (ch. 11)

Such distinctions between Sir Joshua Reynolds and Sir Thomas Lawrence are a Thackeray trademark. Reynolds, the outstanding painter of the eighteenth century, represented that period for him. By contrast, Lawrence, the chief painter of the Regency period in which Thackeray set *Vanity Fair*, stands for a frivolous and dissolute age. With his brilliance and bravura, Lawrence was, for Thackeray, the chronicler of false appearances, the very essence of the age which he so harshly satirised. Dickens too had little time for him; the odious Mr Turveydrop in *Bleak House* permanently poses himself along the lines of Lawrence's private portrait of the Prince Regent.

The account of Bareacres Castle in chapter 49 of *Vanity Fair* is a set-piece expression of Thackeray's views on aristocratic family portraiture. More aware than Dickens of names and styles, Thackeray stresses the rôle of the portrait, both as a register of passing time, and as a form of defiance to it:

> Bareacres Castle . . . with all its costly pictures, furniture, and articles of vertu – the magnificent Vandykes; the noble Reynolds pictures; the Lawrence portraits, tawdry and beautiful, and, thirty years ago, deemed as precious as works of real genius; the matchless Dancing Nymph of Canova, for which Lady Bareacres had sat in her youth – Lady Bareacres splendid then, and radiant in wealth, rank, and beauty – a toothless, bald, old woman now – a mere rag of a former robe of state. Her lord, painted at the same time by Lawrence, as waving his sabre in front of Bareacres Castle, and clothed in his uniform as Colonel of the Thistlewood Yeomanry, was a withered, old, lean man in a great-coat and a Brutus wig, slinking about Gray's Inn of mornings chiefly and dining alone at clubs.

Dickens and Thackeray had both been visitors to country-houses where galleries of family portraits were a prominent feature. George Eliot, whose father was estate manager at Arbury Hall in Warwickshire, was even more familiar with such things. It is to Arbury and its paintings that she refers in 'Mr Gilfil's Love Story' from *Scenes of Clerical Life*, where the Romney portraits of the Newdigates of Arbury gave her a visual parallel for her fictional eighteenth-century characters, the Cheverels. In the story, the portraits (not yet painted at the time of the action) are ascribed to Reynolds. Lady Cheverel is like 'one of Sir Joshua Reynolds's stately ladies, who had suddenly stepped from her frame to enjoy the evening cool' (ch. 2). In the gallery are earlier family portraits, taken at various periods of English history. They establish, like the Dedlock portraits in *Bleak House*, a tradition from which the outsider, Caterina Sarti, feels herself to be excluded.

Later in her life, George Eliot became a visitor to the National Portrait Gallery, opened in 1859 and established for a time in Kensington, where in 1867 she saw displayed portraits from 1688–1800. The visit seems to have influenced the writing of *Daniel Deronda*, with its subtle treatment of portraiture. Deronda, another outsider, stands apart from the Mallinger group and from their portraits. The narrator, however, places him within a less brittle and pretentious tradition, comparing him to the unknown sitter in Titian's *Man with a Glove* (The Louvre), and to the figure of Christ in the same artist's *Tribute Money* (Dresden). His mentor, Mordecai Cohen, is paralleled with Rembrandt's *Man in a Cap* (National Gallery, London). Such metaphors suggest a wide-ranging historical sense, not restricted by national and cultural values like those quoted above. These passages imply that Titian and Rembrandt belong, together with the Jewish tradition, to a morally and socially commendable historical past, while Van Dyck, Gainsborough, and Reynolds (associated with the novel's heroine, Gwendolen Harleth) are rejected along with the English aristocratic world. This contrast raises a number of questions. Is the novelist making a statement about sixteenth-century Venice and seventeenth-century Holland, or is she simply reading her own version of these periods into the paintings? The *Man in a Cap* and the Christ in *The Tribute Money* are comparatively simple figures perhaps, but is the *Man with a Glove* any less aristocratic and arrogant than those people who sat to Reynolds or Van Dyck?

Eighteenth-century portraiture continues to represent a conservative tradition for later novelists. In *The Awkward Age*, published in 1899, Henry James uses the same device to point up the brittle modernity of the Brookenham circle. Mr Longdon, the morally upright man from Suffolk, finds that Mrs Brook quite lacks the old-fashioned virtues of her mother, Lady Julia, an 'absent' character in the novel. When he first sees Nanda Brookenham, Lady Julia's granddaughter, Longdon weeps with emotion at the inherited likeness to Lady Julia. Vanderbank, the young man about town, tells him that Nanda's face 'isn't a bit modern. It's a face of Sir Thomas Lawrence –', but Longdon replies that 'It's a face of Gainsborough! . . . Lady Julia herself harked back' (bk 3, ch. 12). Here again, as in Thackeray, the fashionable Regency artist, Lawrence (to whom Lady Julia might have sat), is rejected in favour of a solid eighteenth-century master. *The Awkward Age* is a satirical and biting novel, reflecting James's unease with the fast world of the *fin de siècle*, and, through Mr Longdon, setting it against the values of the past.

In the twentieth century, few houses have sequences of family portraits, and Virginia Woolf's last novel, *Between the Acts* (1941), comments on this dislocation. The family who once lived in Poyntz Hall have long gone, and the Olivers have bought the house and furnished it with pictures. Even the pair of eighteenth-century portraits do not belong together: 'The lady was a picture, bought by Oliver because he liked the picture; the man was an ancestor. He had a name . . . He was a talk producer, that ancestor. But the lady was a picture' (p. 46). Some of the displaced portraits from places like Poyntz Hall found their way into art galleries, established in increasing numbers after the Napoleonic Wars. From the middle of the nineteenth century, novelists began to make more frequent reference to named artists and works. Limited parallels to family portraiture are replaced by more varied and suggestive references to subject-paintings of all kinds, like George Eliot's use of specific examples from Titian and Rembrandt to describe the appearance of Deronda and Mordecai.

As a young man, just up from the country, Thomas Hardy regularly visited the National Gallery. Some of his most telling metaphors resulted, classic examples of my third category of reference, those which describe a character or event through comparison with a painting. In *The Return of the Native*, for example, Clym Yeobright, after the death of his wife, is said to have the appearance of Sebastiano del Piombo's Lazarus. Angel Clare, in *Tess of the D'Urbervilles*, is compared to Crivelli's *Dead Christ*. These parallels enforce Hardy's sense of the tragedy of the modern world, relating his characters to the structures of religious belief which gave rise to these paintings.

Indeed, the establishment of museums and galleries provided

novelists with a new type of location for fiction, as George Eliot had demonstrated in the Roman scenes of *Middlemarch*. Nathaniel Hawthorne's *The Marble Faun* is an outstanding example of the genre. It begins in the Capitoline Gallery in Rome, and several episodes take place among the city's art collections. There is constant reference to the age of Rome and of its paintings and statues. The dark history of the Papal city is contrasted with the new American world of two of the characters, Hilda, a copyist, and Kenyon, a sculptor. Hilda copies a painting then thought to be by Guido Reni, and erroneously identified as Beatrice Cenci on her way to the scaffold. For Hawthorne, like his contemporaries, the painting was a cult object, and he uses this image as an expression of ancient but equivocal guilt, paralleling the novel's treatment of Rome itself. Beatrice Cenci, victim of rape by her father, whom she murders, is associated with the young artist, Miriam, herself implicated in the murder of a man who dominates her. Hawthorne deepens the parallel by suggesting a likeness between Beatrice and Hilda, whose sight of the crime has destroyed her innocence.

The assumed *Beatrice Cenci* fascinated others. Dickens wrote of it at length in *Pictures from Italy*, and Elizabeth Gaskell refers to it in her account of Mary Barton at the trial of Jem Carson:

> I was not there myself; but one who was, told me that her look, and indeed her whole face, was more like the well-known engraving from Guido's picture of 'Beatrice Cenci' than anything else he could give me an idea of. (ch. 32)

Here Gaskell takes some of the aspects of the painting, the turn of the head, the pathetic expression, the legal processes brought about through a father's guilt. Like Hawthorne, she applies these to a nineteenth-century girl. Mary, who knows that her father is guilty of the murder, shares the complicity in crime of both Miriam and Hilda.

Like Hawthorne, Henry James delighted in the opportunity to place his characters in juxtaposition to works of art. *The American* opens at the Louvre with Christopher Newman in the Salon Carré. The man of the new world, familiar with business, is uneasy: 'Raphael and Titian and Rubens were a new kind of arithmetic, and they inspired our friend, for the first time in his life, with a vague self-mistrust' (ch. 1). Newman's attention is taken by Murillo's *Immaculate Conception*. This most catholic of paintings presents exactly that perplexing ideal of Roman Catholic womanhood which is to ensnare Newman, and which will prevent him from marrying Mme de Cintré. Newman decides to buy a copy from an attractive copyist, part of his attempt to pack up the European past and take it home.

Some of the most subtle 'gallery' scenes are the Dulwich episodes of George Moore's *Evelyn Innes*. Like James and Thackeray, Moore worked as an art critic and reference to painting is a feature in several of his novels. In *Evelyn Innes*, character is frequently revealed through responses to taste and aesthetics. Music is pre-eminent in this respect. Evelyn is a singer and her father a scholar of early music. When she leaves home to become the mistress of a middle-aged connoisseur, Sir Owen Asher, Evelyn fulfils her vocation as an interpreter of modern opera and song. Painting and decorative arts supply a lesser but still important strand in Moore's presentation of his heroine.

Soon after her meeting with Asher, Evelyn takes him to the Dulwich Art Gallery. Looking back, several years later, she believes that two paintings there, *The Colonnade* and *The Lady playing the Virginal*, were symbolic 'of the different lives which had that day pressed upon her choice' (ch. 19).

The second, now known as *Lady with a Clavichord*, is by Gerrit Dou (Moore's Gerard Dow), part of the Dulwich Gallery's extensive collection of seventeenth-century Dutch art. Asher leads Evelyn through these works, telling her that 'Painted by a modern', these works would be

> 'realistic and vulgar; but the Dutchman knew that by light and shade the meanest subject could be made as romantic as a fairy tale. As dreamers and thinkers they did not compare with the Italians, but as painters they were equal to any. They were the first to introduce the trivialities of daily life into Art – the toil of the field, the gross pleasures of the tavern.' (ch. 4)

Asher is an ambivalent character in the novel, sometimes a near caricature of a wealthy hedonist, but his sensitive judgements here are close to Moore's own. His criteria are aesthetic, and he commends the Dutch painters for their treatment of light and shade, and their technical skill:

> 'Look at these boors drinking; they are by Ostade. Are they not admirably drawn and painted? "Brick-making in a Landscape, by Teniers the younger". Won't you look at this? How beautiful! How interesting is its grey sky!'

For Asher, the social aspects of the paintings are subsumed in their painterly qualities. The position which he takes up is quite unlike George Eliot's famous commendation of the human quality of these works in *Adam Bede*.

In the context of Moore's novel, Dutch seventeenth-century art, produce of a world of strict puritanical religion and of worldly comfort, is not appropriate to the life which Asher offers to Evelyn: a brilliant career in *fin de siècle* Paris. As the climax of his tour of the Dutch rooms, however, Asher comes upon a work which lends itself to his purpose:

> 'And here is a Gerard Dow. Miss Innes, will you look at this composition? Is it not admirable? That rich curtain hung across the room, how beautifully painted, how sonorous in colour.'
>
> 'Ah! she's playing a virginal!' said Evelyn, suddenly. 'She is like me, playing and thinking of other things. You can see she is not thinking of the music. She is thinking . . . she is thinking of the world.'
>
> This pleased him, and he said, 'Yes, I suppose it is like your life; it is full of the same romance and mystery.'

The Gerrit Dou painting shows a girl looking out of the picture, while her hands remain upon the keys of the instrument. The objects around her, a cello and a sheet of music, a birdcage, have recently been interpreted as erotic symbols, fitting for the dialogue between Asher and Evelyn. For Moore, however, they are symbols of that domesticity from which Evelyn dreams of escape. Chapter four ends, not as might be expected with this passage, but with a striking and contrasting image. When Evelyn urges a return home, Asher responds: 'Let's look at this picture first – "The Fete beneath the Colonnade" – it is one of the most beautiful things in the world.'

This is *Les Plaisirs du Bal* by the French eighteenth-century artist, Antoine Watteau, who was otherwise unrepresented in British public galleries at this date. In the setting of a grandiloquent loggia, with a poetic landscape opening up beyond, a group of elegant aristocratic figures dance and make love. Asher's comment on the painting is left hanging at the end of the chapter in a tantalising way, but the picture makes two further appearances in the novel. The couple visit the Dulwich Art Gallery again, and on this occasion the scene opens with *Wooded Landscape with a Mill*, by Meindart Hobbema. To Asher it is 'less aggressive than the Colonnade. A sun-lit clearing in a wood and a water mill raised no moral question' (ch. 8). Yet with its image of domestic felicity the picture strikes the wrong moral note for Asher, and he is drawn irresistibly back to the Watteau:

> He turned his eyes back from the dancers, but however he resisted them, their frivolous life found its way into the conversation. They were the wise ones, he said. They lived for art and what else was there in life? A few sonatas, a few operas, a few pictures, a few books, and a love story; we had always to come back to that in the end.

The association of the French rococo masters with sensual and erotic values is a theme of Moore's earlier novel, *A Modern Lover*, in which the struggling artist, Lewis Seymour, produces pastiches of eighteenth-century French art. Seymour's career takes off when he is commissioned to paint murals for an unhappily married woman. Like Owen Asher and Evelyn, the two develop their relationship among works of art, turning over engravings from Boucher and Watteau.

In *Confessions of a Young Man*, Moore writes of these French painters, so closely associated with the *ancien régime*. He probably discovered them through the influential book, *L'Art au Dix-huitième Siècle*, by the brothers Goncourt, itself a source for Walter Pater's 'A Prince of Court Painters' which appeared in 1885. Pater stresses the dark and mysterious side of Watteau's art: 'always a seeker after something in the world that is there in no satisfying measure, or not at all' (*Imaginary Portraits*, 1909, p. 44). By writing of a 'court painter', Pater defied those traditional attitudes, which condemned the eighteenth-century French court and its painters as frivolous and meretricious.

Evelyn chooses Asher and with him the hedonistic world of Paris, where she makes her name as a great singer. When, years later, she returns to London, Asher creates an eighteenth-century drawing-room for her, following the example of some of the great collectors of his time. Moore carefully introduces the precise details of this room into the text. The clock (with a muse and a cupid) belongs to the era of Louis XV, the carpet is Aubusson, the sofa Sheraton, the bowls Worcester. The effect is completed with a work by Boucher, of a 'woman lying on her stomach, drawn very freely, very simply – quite a large drawing – just the thing for such a room as hers' (ch. 12).

When Evelyn begins to reject Asher and his world, she turns to an Irishman, Ulick Dean (based upon W. B. Yeats). When she asks Dean his opinion of *Les Plaisirs du Bal*, he interprets the painting as a charade: 'Their thoughts . . . are not in their evening parade; something quite different is happening in their hearts' (ch. 19).

If prepared to admit that Evelyn's Boucher is 'graceful', Dean tells her that Michaelangelo and Leonardo are more to his own taste. He praises an 'eighteenth-century mystic', William Blake, in whose work 'passion of the flesh' is not 'destitute of spiritual exaltation'. Blake is an idealist and visionary, while, for Dean, the objects surrounding Evelyn are products of a frivolous and wealthy aristocratic society.

Moore's references to painting in *Evelyn Innes* are never mechanical. *Les Plaisirs du Bal* is a masterpiece, and it retains its mystery for the novel's characters, posing questions and supplying no answers. Watteau's world is inaccessible to them, but the high society to which Evelyn belongs has its own artificialities and conventions.

If reference to painting can open up the past, suggesting fruitful connections with the present, the technique does have limitations. Not all readers will recognise the names or styles, and painting itself is often the preserve of a minority. Among the examples mentioned in this essay, none has been concerned with the uncultured or the plebeian. Emile Zola made a rare, and successful, attempt to achieve this in *L'Assommoir*, where Gervaise Coupeau's wedding party manages to lose itself in the Louvre, while filling in the time before dinner. Beginning in the French Gallery, they are impressed by Géricault's enormous *Raft of the Medusa*. In the Salon Carré the bride asks about the subject of Veronese's *Marriage Feast at Cana*, a sumptuous and worldly scene quite unlike her own wedding breakfast. The bridegroom decides that *Mona Lisa* is like his aunt, and another guest, whose wife is pregnant, stands before the same Murillo *Virgin* which fascinated Newman, with his mouth open. When they become exhausted, they march from room to room and school to school, uncomprehendingly passing centuries of painting. Only the scatological details of Rubens's *Kermesse* can hold their attention, before they retrace their steps, desperately searching for a way out. For this fictional group at least, history and art are all one meaningless blur.

Waverley and the Battle of Culloden

CLAIRE LAMONT

Walter Scott's first novel, *Waverley*, is set in the years 1744–46 and deals with the rising on behalf of the Jacobite claimant to the throne of George II known as 'the '45'. The decisive battle of those years was that at Culloden in April 1746 where the Jacobites were finally defeated.[1] A battle is presented in *Waverley*; but it is not Culloden. The battle that occurs in the novel is that fought at Prestonpans in September 1745, which was a Jacobite victory. Culloden is conspicuously absent. My purpose in what follows is to ask what is the consequence for our reading of *Waverley* of the subordination of the battle of Culloden?

Waverley was published in 1814 in three volumes. The first volume ends with chapters in which the young English hero, Edward Waverley, is introduced to the traditional and Jacobite culture of the Scottish Highlands in the household of the clan chieftain Fergus Mac-Ivor. The second volume ends with chapters describing the battle of Prestonpans in which Prince Charles Stuart with his Highland followers defeated a Hanoverian army. It is in the third volume that the balance of power shifts from the Jacobites to the Hanoverians. The Jacobites had entered Edinburgh and established Prince Charles at Holyrood, the palace of his ancestors. But they had never entirely captured the city: the Hanoverian garrison of Edinburgh Castle held out. Jacobite rejoicing is disturbed by the periodic eruption of canon-fire from the Castle. The future of Scotland, if not of Britain, is in the balance as the opposing sides hold the two symbolic sites which mark the extremities of the High Street of Edinburgh, Holyrood Palace to the east and Edinburgh Castle to the west, right of birth versus actual power. As those holding the Castle are gradually revealed to be invincible, the fortunes of the Jacobites start to turn. Ominously, the march into England is undertaken only when the Jacobites weary of besieging the Castle.

1 Walter Scott, *Tales of a Grandfather*, 3rd series (Edinburgh, 1830), vols II and III; John Prebble, *Culloden* (London, 1961); Bruce Lenman, *The Jacobite Risings in Britain 1689–1746* (London, 1980); Jeremy Black, *Culloden and the '45*, (Stroud, 1990).

It is in volume II, chapter 17 that Edward Waverley finds himself at the court of Prince Charles at Holyrood on the eve of the march which led to the battle of Prestonpans. Waverley joins the Jacobite army, and the novel then follows that army to the battle and on its subsequent march into England. On the retreat from Derby the Jacobites were involved in a skirmish at Clifton, near Penrith, where in the novel Fergus Mac-Ivor is captured and Waverley is separated from the army in the dark and confusion. Between volume II, chapter 17 and volume III, chapter 12 the progress of the Jacobite army is followed through Waverley's participation in their march. (Although one has to notice that neither his joining it nor his leaving it is premeditated). Once Waverley is separated from the army we do not hear directly of its fate. It was a bitter one. The army retreated further and further north. It won a defensive battle at Falkirk; and then was crushingly defeated at Culloden, near Inverness.

The battle of Culloden, the last battle on British soil, was fought on 16 April 1746. It was a defeat from which Jacobitism as a political force never recovered. But the significance of the battle for the Highlands of Scotland was not just that it was a defeat; it was a defeat after which the victor took particularly savage vengeance against his opponents. The fright that the episode had given to the government in London caused it to follow Culloden with a series of measures designed, by destroying the culture from which such unruly forces had erupted, to prevent any repetition. When one mentions Culloden one refers not only to a battle, but also to its savage aftermath, and to painful social consequences for Highland Scotland in the decades that followed.

It could be argued that a historical novelist setting a work in 1744–46 might consciously try to avoid dealing with the consequences of a battle, and might invite the reader to see these years as an island of time. But that is prevented in *Waverley* by the device of the narrator – albeit a vestigial narrator in comparison with Scott's later ones. This narrator self-consciously starts his novel on 1 November 1805,[2] and after a semi-humorous rehearsal of the options gives it the subtitle *'Tis Sixty Years Since* (pp. 3–4). These indications of the date of writing, not to mention several subsequent interpositions by the narrator, bring into the novel the gap in time since the events it describes took place.

2 Walter Scott, *Waverley; or, 'Tis Sixty Years Since*, ed. Claire Lamont (Oxford, 1981), p. 4; hereafter by page references in the text.

The treatment of Culloden in the novel cannot be explained by supposing the narrator unaware of the implications of his subtitle.

My concern is with the ending of the novel. The tale is told from the point of the hero. At the end he receives a pardon from the government and marries the simpler and less heroic of the two heroines. The end of *Waverley* seems to be concerned with reconciliation and reconstruction, and with marriage as a symbol of harmony restored. Does the reader in the midst of this remember Culloden?

Scott's historical novels commonly bring together a romance plot and a historical theme. It is not therefore surprising that the moment of closure should present some difficulty. A reading of the end of *Waverley* that finds its closure satisfactory is one which concentrates on the romance plot of the novel. According to that reading a young man sets out on his first adventure into the adult world. He is seduced by his romantic tastes into offering his service to Flora Mac-Ivor and Prince Charles Stuart. After living through the painful consequences of these allegiances, he finds himself 'A sadder and a wiser man' (p. 296). He hopes 'that it might never again be his lot to draw his sword in civil conflict' (p. 283) and discovers the domestic side of his character with Rose Bradwardine. The ending of the novel is full of episodes implying closure: the marriage of Edward and Rose; the repair of Tully-Veolan, the house damaged by the civil war; the reclothing of the poor retainer, Davie Gellatly, who had been left destitute during the fighting. The old paintings in the house, used by the invading soldiers for target-practice (p. 297), are replaced by this:

> a large and spirited painting, representing Fergus Mac-Ivor and Waverley in their Highland dress, the scene a wild, rocky, and mountainous pass, down which the clan were descending in the background. (p. 338)

Waverley's arms, given him by Prince Charles, are set on the mantelpiece as an ornament (pp. 196, 338). These elements of the narrative all have one tendency, they endorse and celebrate peace. But they do more than that. They seem to rejoice in the loss of certain features of the old Scotland. The fact that the soldiers had burned 'the stables and out-houses' at Tully-Veolan is seen as a good opportunity to replace them with 'buildings of a lighter and more picturesque appearance' (pp. 296, 334). We are now moving into a culture in which the proper place for a sword is a mantelpiece. The place for young men in tartan is in paintings. This 'symbolic' reading of the ending of the novel projects the mind into the future. It celebrates prospectively the peace and prosperity to come to Scotland through the defeat of the Jacobites. The new Hanoverian world will treat the old Scottish culture as a romantic ornament. The future dimension of its symbolism is betrayed by the narrator's compliment to the painter of the portrait of Fergus and Waverley:

> Raeburn himself, (whose Highland Chiefs do all but walk out of the canvas) could not have done more justice to the subject; and the ardent, fiery, and impetuous character of the unfortunate Chief of Glennaquoich was finely contrasted with the contemplative, fanciful, and enthusiastic expression of his happier friend. (p. 338)

Henry Raeburn was born in 1756; his portraits of clan chiefs are of Scott's period, not of the 1740s. This interpretation might be called humanist in that it seeks to find satisfactory strategies of closure, is willing to see large themes mediated through the individual, and sees the novel as making a positive comment on life. But can the symbolic reading of the end of the novel as a celebration of peace and prosperity be sustained if the reader remembers the other theme of the novel, not the romance but the history?

To remember the historical theme is to deconstruct the romance ending. While the romance plot of the novel is being rounded off in a series of positive symbols, what is the fate of the Jacobites? Waverley is separated from the Jacobite army at Clifton, and as he lies in hiding in Cumberland news filters through to him of the Jacobite retreat and the battle of Falkirk. When a few months later he reached the borders of Scotland,

> he heard the tidings of the decisive battle of Culloden. It was no more than he had long expected, though the success at Falkirk had thrown a faint and setting gleam over the arms of the Chevalier. Yet it came upon him like a shock, by which he was for a time altogether unmanned. The generous, the courteous, the noble-minded Adventurer, was then a fugitive, with a price upon his head; his adherents, so brave, so enthusiastic, so faithful, were dead, imprisoned, or exiled. (p. 293)

A friendly Edinburgh landlady gives him news of Fergus Mac-Ivor, which she had heard from one of his followers:

> 'The poor Hieland body, Dugald Mahony, cam here a while since

> wi'ane o' his arms cut off, and a sair clour in the head – ye'll mind Dugald, he carried aye an axe on his shouther – and he cam here just begging, as I may say, for something to eat.' (p. 294)

Waverley asks about his other friends, and she replies, 'Ou, wha kens where ony o'them is now? puir things, they're sair ta'en down for their white cockades and their white roses' (p. 295). Waverley soon sees the consequences of war for himself:

> As he advanced northward, the traces of war became visible. Broken carriages, dead horses, unroofed cottages, trees felled for palisades, and bridges destroyed, or only partially repaired; all indicated the movements of hostile armies. In those places where the gentry were attached to the Stuart cause, their houses seemed dismantled or deserted, the usual course of what may be called ornamental labour was totally interrupted, and the inhabitants were seen gliding about with fear, sorrow, and dejection in their faces. (p. 295)

Waverley visits Fergus Mac-Ivor in prison in Carlisle on the morning of the day on which he was to suffer the penalty for high treason. The chieftain recommends his clansmen to Waverley's protection:

> '. . . when you hear of these poor Mac-Ivors being distressed about their miserable possessions by some harsh overseer or agent of government, remember that you have worn their tartan, and are an adopted son of their race.' (p. 325)

And he adds, 'Would to God . . . I could bequeath to you my rights to the love and obedience of this primitive and brave race' (p. 325).

The bitter social consequences of the defeat of the Jacobites are certainly not omitted from *Waverley*. The end of the novel, however, gives diminishing attention to them. The novel turns away from the Highlanders in a post-Culloden world to present us with Waverley's marriage, his newly restored furniture, and his pictures. We are not invited to consider that possession of the arms which Waverley places on the mantelpiece would have been illegal under the Disarming Act of 1746. The end of the novel puts side by side an individual's achievement of responsible adulthood and measures designed to destroy a culture. The two come together awkwardly. Tully-Veolan is speedily repaired. It is restored by waving a wand – or as the Baron suggests by 'brownies and fairies' (p. 339). The reader of the historical plot knows that the wand, if it was not entirely out of the world of romance, was a southerner's money, and that there was no such wand in the rest of the Highlands. The problem is that the romance theme looks forwards, and the historical theme looks backwards to what has been destroyed, and the end of the novel risks a clash between them.

It may be objected that the novel has to proceed by metonymy, letting the part stand for the whole. It cannot be said that Scott flinched from introducing into his novel the horror of civil war, and the atrocity with which the '45 was suppressed. The death of Fergus Mac-Ivor by the horrible death for high treason is sufficient evidence that the novel does not seek to deny suffering. Surely Scott has represented the violence and loss of the '45, and the novel is allowed to end with celebration and hope for the future? The trouble is that the history of the novel has established itself with a remorseless continuum which will not allow itself to be forgotten: Prestonpans, Derby, Clifton, Falkirk . . . Who cares about the recovery of the Blessed Bear of Bradwardine, the Baron's favourite drinking-cup, in the aftermath of Culloden? Once you have mentioned the penalty for high treason (which was hanging, drawing, and quartering) and the battle of Culloden, the positive symbols which close the romance plot are seriously undermined.

This interpretation of the ending of *Waverley* has not been a dominant one, but it has been there from the beginning. A reviewer in the *Caledonian Mercury*, an Edinburgh newspaper with a Jacobite ancestry, on 29 October 1814 wrote this, after mentioning the death of Fergus Mac-Ivor:

> But the reader, wholly absorbed in the interest of the preceding scenes, which are indeed nobly described, turns with some degree of aversion from the story of Waverley's marriage, and the merriment by which it is followed. The fate of the unfortunate Chieftain, and his faithful companion Evan Dhu – their heroism in suffering, and their noble contempt of death, with all its tragical apparatus, leaves the mind in too solemn a mood to follow so trifling a character as Waverley through the lighter scenes of this prosperous life.

The difference between these two readings of the end of *Waverley* is the difference between criticism written from the supposed point of view of the writer and that written from the point of view of the reader. The writer is in one account free to choose where to start and end the narrative, to substitute one act of violence for another, and to end with symbolic episodes which look further forward than the period in which they are set. The reader in the other account is free to dislike the result. And the reader is more likely to dislike the result in an historical novel than in one that is not apparently historical, because in such a novel the reader is part-possessor of the subject-matter. There is the risk of a clash at the end of *Waverley* between the romance plot, which ends optimistically, and the historical theme, which ends tragically. For some readers at least, what they know about the history, the narrative of the nation, clashes with the narrative of Edward Waverley. The sovereignty of the author over history works only where either the reader does not know the history or is willing to see it reinterpreted. Most audiences of Shakespeare's history plays do not know where he has altered history. The only difficulty comes when they do, and when they refuse to yield their interpretation to his. There are those who will not accept his presentation of, for instance, Joan of Arc or Richard III. In historical fiction at least, history is what you remember. And many people remember the '45. For those who do, the end of *Waverley* is not just forward-looking symbolism, it looks dangerously like Whig propaganda.

The argument so far has derived an unsatisfactory pair of alternatives from the conclusion of *Waverley*: either the romance ending is imposed on history or the history mars the romance ending. A way out of this dilemma is shown by Mary Lascelles in a passage which reconciles the claims of both writer and reader. In her book on historical fiction, *The Story-Teller Retrieves the Past* (Oxford, 1980), she writes:

> The marriage of history with invented narrative poses its own problems. History will accept romance as partner, if the reader will but withdraw his critical faculties from the conclusion, as Scott requires. This is a comfortable convention, and, if we are inclined to demur at such a regard for our comfort, we shall not be reading this kind of book. Nevertheless, it shows a want of literary good manners in the writer if he treats a grave historical situation otherwise than seriously, before this separation of the partners, as it were by mutual agreement, frees him from any such obligation. (p. 76)

This presents the reading of historical fiction of Scott's type as a bargain between reader and novelist. The reader must 'withdraw his critical faculties' at the end. Such withdrawal is assisted by the unique bookishness of the novel as a genre: readers of the conventionally-published novel have always been able to see, by the small number of pages left, how close they are to the end, and make adjustments to their reading accordingly. Under this interpretation the reader acquiesces in the constraints imposed by both novel and book.

Does *Waverley* help us to read its ending? To borrow terminology from Wolfgang Iser, what is there in the structuring of the text which would 'imply' the reader of its conclusion? Iser addresses the problem of the conclusion of *Waverley*:

> While the hero's function is to bring past reality to life, history itself does not come to any end – as Scott's subtitle indicates – and so the novel can only come to a stop if the main figure once more steps into the foreground. But this would mean a total change of emphasis as regards the subject matter of the novel, with Waverley taking precedence over events and history supplying only the trappings for the hero's development. Scott deals with this problem by adopting an ironic style in depicting his hero at the end.[3]

Iser suggests that irony in Scott's description of Waverley's marriage deflects attention away from the hero and on to history. (He does not say anything about the significance of that history; history may not come to an end, but it is not an uninflected continuum). There is certainly irony in the last chapters of the novel, the sort of irony appropriate to bystanders at a wedding, and to a narrator closing a novel with conventional symbols. But does such irony have the effect of leaving 'historical reality . . . properly situated in the foreground'? I suggest on the contrary that the attention of the novel is not directed back to the historical theme at its end, because in the 'prestructuring of the potential meaning'[4] of the conclusion some techniques of closure have already been applied to the historical theme.

In writing historical fiction Scott established a model which has been followed by many later historical novelists: his historical characters make brief but significant appearances. The hero or heroine, and the other leading characters are fictitious. If the novel is to have Queen Elizabeth, Oliver Cromwell, or Prince Charles Stuart in it, Scott will ensure that the scenes where they appear are brief, intense, and self-contained. In *Waverley* the focus on history is comparably treated. The subtitle indicates the period at which the novel is set. Beyond that, time is only vaguely indicated during the first two volumes. Waverley leaves Waverley-Honour to join the army in Scotland

3 Wolfgang Iser, *The Implied Reader: Patterns of Communication in Prose Fiction from Bunyan to Beckett* (Baltimore and London, 1974), p. 98.

4 Iser, p. xii.

in the Autumn of 1744 (pp. 4–5, 22). 'The arrival of summer' caused him to visit Tully-Veolan (p. 31). When the Jacobite army gathered in King's Park, Edinburgh, 'the autumn was now waning, and the nights beginning to be frosty' (p. 212). The famous dates of the summer of 1745 are not mentioned: Prince Charles raised his standard at Glenfinnan on 19 August and entered Edinburgh on 17 September. The dating in the novel is perhaps too reticent for those who do not know the succession of events in the '45; slight hints are enough for those who do. The battle of Prestonpans is described in detail at the end of volume II, and the historicity of it is stressed by the mention of the first of a series of dates marking the Jacobite campaign of the autumn of 1745 (p. 239).[5] The Jacobites began their march into England 'about the beginning of November' (p. 263); the retreat was determined upon on 5 December (p. 274); and the skirmish at Clifton occurred on 18 December (p. 274). From then on there are only slight indications of time passing, and that time is passed in the story of Edward Waverley. It is only incidentally and without dates that we hear of the events of 1746, the battle of Falkirk (17 January) and Culloden (16 April). Waverley needs time to make the sober reflections which are part of his growing-up process; but that time cannot be measured against the stern calendar of 1746. In the novel, history and romance come together for the second half of 1745. After that, history recedes into the background and there are no specific time references. The time at the end of the novel is personal time, not historic time. At its end the novel moves out of the orbit of history, and many readers have made no demur.

What I have referred to as the end of the novel starts at volume III, chapter 23. It is the chapter after the death of Fergus Mac-Ivor and it starts with a passage of transition from history to romance, and from content to closure:

> The impression of horror with which Waverley left Carlisle, softened by degrees into melancholy, a gradation which was accelerated by the painful, yet soothing, task of writing to Rose; and, while he

5 The date is given as 'the 20th'. The battle of Prestonpans was fought early on the morning of 21 September 1745. Scott's error probably arose from a sentence in the book he was consulting for the details of the battle, John Home, *The History of the Rebellion in the year 1745* (London, 1802), p. 112. It is curious that Scott does not give the month, which was September; presumably an oversight, unless he expected his reader to know it or thought the reference to frosty autumn weather told all that was needed.

> could not suppress his own feelings of the calamity, by endeavouring to place it in a light which might grieve her, without shocking her imagination. The picture which he drew for her benefit he gradually familiarized to his own mind, and his next letters were more cheerful, and referred to the prospects of peace and happiness which lay before them. (p. 329)

This is a short history of survival. Without going fully into the delicate distinction that Scott makes in the words 'which might grieve her, without shocking her imagination', it could be said that the death of Fergus is described in a way to make it endurable. The description intended for Rose is then adopted by Waverley himself. The placing of the passage seems to indicate that the reader is invited to accept it too.

I have tried to describe some ways in which the end of *Waverley* might be read. One cannot do so, however, without reflecting on just what historical event it was that Scott subordinated at the end of the novel, the battle of Culloden.

Scott's own views are well enough known. He declared himself to have been 'a valiant Jacobite at the age of ten years old'.[6] In his autobiographical fragment he wrote, after mentioning Culloden: 'One or two of our own distant relations had fallen on that occasion, and I remember detesting the name of Cumberland [the Hanoverian commander] with more than infant hatred.'[7] In adult life his judgement 'inclined for the public weal to the present succession', but he never swore the oaths required of magistrates, which involved 'abjuring the Pretender', without 'a qualm of conscience'.[8] In his fiction, *Waverley* is the nearest he ever came to writing about the battle of Culloden. Of his other Jacobite novels, *Rob Roy* (1817) is set earlier in the century; *Redgauntlet* (1824) and *The Highland Widow* (1827) later. He did, however, write about Culloden in his non-fiction, in two reviews[9] and in the history of Scotland which he wrote for his grandson, *Tales of a Grandfather*.

6 In a letter to Robert Surtees, 17 December, 1806: *The Letters of Sir Walter Scott*, ed. H. J. C. Grierson (London, 1932–7), *Letters 1787–1808*, p. 343.

7 J. G. Lockhart, *Memoirs of the Life of Sir Walter Scott, Bart.* (Edinburgh, 1837–8), I, 18.

8 In a letter to Margaret Clephane, 13 July, 1813: *Letters 1811–1814*, pp. 302–3.

9 In his reviews of *The Culloden Papers* and of *The Life and Works of John Home* in *The Quarterly Review*, XIV, 1816, and XXXVI, 1827.

Despite the fact that it was 'Sixty Years Since' (almost seventy by the date of publication) the '45 was not an easy matter to treat in a novel. The reviewer for *The Antijacobin Review* noted that 'the writer takes upon himself a task of peculiar delicacy, and attended with peculiar difficulty.' The delicacy was caused by the possibility of a lingering sensitivity to the political loyalties displayed in the novel. The reviewer congratulates the novelist:

> The author, however, has performed this difficult task with considerable skill and ability, steering clear of every thing which could give offence to the reigning family, and yet not disgracing himself by the sacrifice of truth, or by the abject servility of a time-serving parasite.[10]

By the time Scott wrote, various ways of referring to the '45 had been established. Whig rejoicing at the removal of the threat to the Hanoverian succession had been countered by the development of the Jacobite lyric, to which Burns made a distinguished contribution, in which the defeated Prince is described in the highly-charged language of love-poetry.[11] In *Waverley*, Scott side-steps this tradition: he presents a picture of the Jacobite claimant which is both sympathetic and astringent. The novel is not Jacobite in the political sense: it does not wish for a different monarch nor does it romanticise the dispossessed heir. The much-romanticised escape of the Prince after Culloden is alluded to only in the briefest manner in *Waverley* (p. 325). The way that the battle of Culloden was described in the late eighteenth century depended on the politics of the writer. To illustrate one can compare the Whig travel writer, Thomas Pennant, and the Tory, Samuel Johnson. Here is Pennant describing his visit to Culloden: 'Passed over *Culloden Moor*, the place that *North Britain* owes its present prosperity to, by the victory of April 16, 1746.'[12] After a reference to the aftermath of the battle he remarks: 'But let a veil be flung over a few excesses consequential of a day, productive of so much benefit to the united kingdoms.' Johnson's travel book about Scotland was written partly in answer to Pennant. In his reflections on the condition of the Highlanders in 1773, the year of his tour, he sees them as a

10 *The Antijacobin Review*, XLVII (1814), p. 218.

11 William Donaldson, *The Jacobite Song: Political Myth and National Identity* (Aberdeen, 1988).

12 Thomas Pennant, A *Tour in Scotland* MDCCLXIX (London, 1771), p. 158.

conquered people: 'Their pride has been crushed by the heavy hand of a vindictive conqueror'.[13] Yet his references to Culloden itself are reticent. Restraint, almost silence, is perceptible in both Johnson and Scott when writing of the battle which signalised the change they record in Highland society. There is in the work of both writers *then* and *now*, and reticence over what caused the difference between them.

This sense of a watershed is present in Scott's Jacobite works which are set after 1745. In both *Redgauntlet* and *The Highland Widow* there are indomitable characters who seek to deny the realities of the post-Culloden world; in both works, the younger generation has to try to come to terms with the world as it is. A momentous event in the past divides the generations. In *Waverley*, Scott's first novel, he came dangerously near to that event to which he elsewhere only alludes. When he took Jacobite subject-matter in later works he distanced it so that he merely had to indicate a source in the past of grief and dispossession, one which is the more powerful for being indicated rather than specified.

Culloden is Scott's watershed. And it is largely absent from his fiction. In *Waverley*, Scott presents a pre-Culloden view of the Highlands. Reviewers noticed that, and appreciated it.[14] They too did not allude to what had destroyed this world. The reader of *Waverley* is not simply reading about a society outside his or her experience; but a society that once was and no longer is. The novel is reticent about the battle of Culloden, but because of the vantage point of narrator and reader sixty or more years later, the silence is eloquent. It is out of the silence, and the gap in time, that the subject-matter comes, the loss of a culture. The unspoken in *Waverley* is heavy with mythical significance.

Waverley was published in 1814. Romanticism is frequently described as giving renewed value to traditional cultures. Scott in *Waverley* portrayed the paradigmatic destroyed culture. He presented Highland Scotland to our consciousness as Troy had been to the classical world: as the value-charged place which was destroyed.

13 Samuel Johnson, *A Journey to the Western Islands of Scotland*, ed. Mary Lascelles (Yale Edition of the Works of Samuel Johnson, New Haven, 1971), p. 89.

14 E.g., the reviewer in the *British Critic*, ns II (1814), pp. 189–211; and Francis Jeffrey in the *Edinburgh Review*, XXIV (1814), pp. 208–43; both reprinted in John O. Hayden, *Scott: The Critical Heritage* (London, 1970), pp. 68–9 and 80.

Scott's contribution to the modern consciousness was to write what hostile commentators present as a small rebellion-turned-civil-war as a modern myth. It was the story of the Europe of the Napoleonic wars, and is the story in perhaps all the continents in the modern world, where the history of the dominant culture is written on top of the unwritten histories of the smaller cultures it defeated. I started by suggesting that the question of the battle of Culloden depended on how we read a historical novel. I suggest now that it is a matter of how the novel reads the modern world. The 'absent' battle of Culloden is the fact that is most centrally present in *Waverley*.

A Novel Scarcely Historical? *Time and History in Dickens's* Little Dorrit

ANGUS EASSON

When in chapter 12 of *Little Dorrit* Arthur Clennam first goes to Bleeding Heart Yard, the place is introduced by its history, though the glory is departed, now that it is absorbed in London and no longer boasts, as in Shakespeare's time, royal hunting seats, however there may still be 'some relish of ancient greatness about it', amidst which dwell its impoverished inhabitants, 'as the Arabs of the desert pitch their tents among the fallen stones of the Pyramids'.[1] The imagined temporal vista that stretches back to the Pharoahs suggests a world fallen from the splendour that was Egypt, even from the more recent yet golden days of Shakespeare, one in which men have lost the secret of engineering feats like the Pyramids, have dwindled, while in the pleasures of the chase, no spot is left there now but for hunters of men. This sense of camping out in splendours ruinous and too large for their present usurpers is repeated later in the Italian scenes of the novel and contributes to that perspective of history in the novel which presents a world fallen and degenerated, darkened from the hunting of game to the hunting of men.

History as an understanding of the past and of its evidences is found in the Yard too. The explanations of the name, Bleeding Heart Yard, seem to offer an account of, even while their fictiveness mocks, the past: one party favours a murder, another (including all the gentler sex) a love story, though the girl's refrain, 'Bleeding Heart, Bleeding Heart, bleeding away', has the objection against it of being the invention of a tambour-worker still lodging in the Yard. Both parties though reject the antiquarian explanation of a feudal cognisance (p. 177) and the narrator, whatever his scepticism, thinks them right to reject Dryasdust who would despoil them of their one little grain of poetry sparkling in the coarse sand that ran through 'the hour glass they turned from year to year' (p. 177). The Yarders imaginatively charge

1 *Little Dorrit*, ed. John Holloway (Penguin English Library; now Penguin Classics) (Harmondsworth, 1967; 1973), p. 176; hereafter page references in the text are to this edition.

the world in which they live by projections from their present selves. They tie themselves in with here and now to deliver what they can of a golden world rather than the brazen of the historian.

Bleeding Heart Yard might seem to exemplify the various nature of history: an area of the past, which has existed; an area of the past which is described, whether by narrator or antiquarian; an explanation of the past. Yet for all the passage's insistence upon these versions of history, it remains true that the Yarders are not of this past and their perspective on it is essentially ahistorical. It is invention and poetry that touches them, not a sense of continuity with that past, and the tambour-maker lodges in the Yard still, in the narrative's present, a poet rather than a historian. And if, being of these latter days, these people are the present prey of the hunters of men, of Pancks and his master Casby, the account that places those days of royal hunting seats in a remote and separate era asserts, in its sneering reference to Shakespeare as 'stage-player', Dickens's own mid nineteenth-century concern for the dignity of literature through an author who will 'always be remembered with pride and veneration by the civilised world'.[2] Shakespeare abides, while the hunting seats recede with the stones of the Pyramids and the ruins of Rome.

Such a complex of ideas on history is one way into considering the 'historical' nature of *Little Dorrit*, or whether indeed its nature is historical. As already suggested, even when ostensibly representing the past or interpretations of the past, its sense of the present is strong. The account of Bleeding Heart Yard suggests a gap in time over which we regard that 'other', which is history, the golden but alien age, while all on this side is the present. Indeed, it is usual, and on good grounds, to treat *Little Dorrit* as a novel dealing with the contemporary rather than with the historical. Sometimes it would almost seem that *Little Dorrit* is only historical in the sense that our temporal situation makes it so for us. Bleeding Heart Yard might be a paradigm of the novel's crowding towards the present. Even as history is invoked, Dickens draws this passage close to the present moment of 1855 in which he writes it. Not only is there allusion to the dignity of literature, but that hourglass and its golden grains echoes *Hard Times* (1854), subtitled 'For These Times', with its claim for fancy in a world of uniformity and toil, as it echoes too Dickens's concern in the campaigning journalism of *Household Words* for social welfare and social action.

Since the contemporaneity of *Little Dorrit* has been so much

2 Charles Dickens, *A Child's History of England*, ch. 31.

stressed, I want to redress the balance by looking at questions of history in the novel, even though I begin in the 1850s. Certainly, few readers then and few now are surprised by *Little Dorrit*'s sense of the present moment, despite the novel's arresting opening claim to be a narrative of the past: 'Thirty years ago, Marseilles lay burning in the sun, one day' (p. 39); despite too the way it roves back another twenty to Mr Dorrit's entry into the Marshalsea, and despite the way that Dorrit's life, like the forty-year-old Clennam's, must begin in the eighteenth century. *Little Dorrit*'s contemporaneity can be established in a number of ways. It is clear from Dickens's letters, journalism, and speeches that the public events of 1854 and 1855 – cholera, the Crimean War, administrative incompetence – deeply affected him and deeply affected the writing of the novel. Writing to Austin Henry Layard, who was leading the Parliamentary attack upon Administrative incompetence, Dickens said (10 April 1855) he detected a mood in the people of increasing resentment, like that before the first French Revolution, at their 'alienation . . . from their own public affairs', which threatened the whole social fabric. The prominence of political, social, and ethical themes, shadowed in Phiz's cover design for the serial numbers, has been discussed by John Butt and Kathleen Tillotson in 'From "Nobody's Fault" to *Little Dorrit*'.[3]

For the original readers, in December 1855, the novel's opening in France, quite apart from the euphony between Marseilles and that other prison of the Marshalsea, would be topical enough, since Great Britain and France had been allies since early 1854 in the Crimean War, while 1854 and 1855 had seen a flurry of reciprocal royal visits, and May 1855 the opening of the Paris Universal Exhibition, which ran until the late autumn. The Marseilles quarantine would remind the contemporary reader of the modern scourge of Asiatic cholera that had ravaged Britain in 1854, whole sections of London being cordoned off, rather than of the mediaeval spectre of the Black Death, while the London Sunday that greets Clennam, where the bells ring as though the plague were in the city (as it had been only a year before), is closed to refreshment of body or mind for the ordinary citizen as firmly in the style of the 1850s as anything of the 1820s. The Beer Act of 1854 that closed public houses on Sundays to all except 'bona fide' travellers, and Lord Robert Grosvenor's Prevention of Sunday Trading Bill (a measure that would oppress the poor while not affecting the

3 *Dickens at Work*, 1957, pp. 222–33.

rich and provoked riots in Hyde Park) threatened a Sunday not only without entertainment but also without opportunity for the working man to buy food or drink after toiling six days. The 1850s promised to be as oppressive as anything proposed earlier in the century.

If *Little Dorrit* can be taken as a novel about the 1850s, a history of its own times perhaps, but if so in that limited sense only, then its relation to Dickens's personal history might also be considered. *Little Dorrit* can be read as in some measure an autobiographical projection. If public events provoked the novel, private episodes stirred Dickens strongly too. Dickens, at forty-two, though without the wasted years of Clennam, had met again, in early 1855, his first love, Maria Beadnell, now Mrs Winter, and while the Dora of *David Copperfield*, a version of that early love, is transmogrified into the comic warm-hearted Flora Finching, strains in Dickens's marriage, beginning to show about this time and which reached the crisis of separation three years later, may well have been aggravated by this revival of his past and his youth, however grotesque the contrast between Maria and Mrs Winter. In 1854 and 1855, Dickens was also showing signs of overwork (the strain, not the work itself, was unusual) and was often angry, even to helplessness, at the turn of public events: progress in education, sanitation, social reconciliation, scant enough, was further impeded by the Crimean war (an excuse to defer home legislation), while the conduct of the war itself seemed increasingly criminal, with an army before Sebastopol virtually abandoned by the government and destroyed less by the enemy than by disease, lack of supplies, and general incompetence (it was another humiliation, felt deeply and not by Dickens alone, that the French ordered these things better, as was bitterly obvious to observers in the Crimea). Little wonder then at Dickens's delight in reporting to Wilkie Collins (30 September 1855) that 'I have relieved my indignant soul with a scarifier', in writing chapter 10, 'Containing the Whole Science of Government'.

Yet such anger and distress, while clearly written into (and controlled within) the novel, available to the modern reader and Dickens's friends and readable at a general level by his contemporary audience, is not at a high level of auto-specificity. We would not expect Dickens to be explicit about his private life in fiction, nor would we expect him anachronistically to include the Crimean War, though coded versions might have appeared. Dickens's particularity of satire might easily have seized on the notorious 'green coffee' affair, just as he later seized on the financier Sadleir as a model for Mr Merdle. Coffee provided for the Crimea was being sent out to men who after long hours of duty and with scant fuel were meant to both roast and grind the beans. Yet what is remarkable about the Circumlocution satire is its generality, not its specificity of detail.

On the other hand, if history is taken primarily as the story of the past, then the Marshalsea prison, which Mr Dorrit enters in 1805, offered a very specific historical opportunity for Dickens to record something of himself. Here, in 1824, his father had been imprisoned, while he himself was found work in the Blacking Warehouse. Those of Dickens's circle who knew of this Marshalsea episode were few: – John Forster and Mrs Dickens, perhaps no more in 1855. And indeed, even with our biographical hindsight, it is difficult to catch any particular hint in the writing of that childhood trauma. The prison is presented without bitterness nor is there any structurally inexplicable emphasis (such as occurs at the opening of chapter 11 of *David Copperfield*, where Dickens interposes his self over David's family situation) that might be the tracer of personal significance.[4] Certainly, the prison is presented powerfully and its nature stressed by Little Dorrit in its midst, the child of the Marshalsea, strong Cordelia to the weak Lear of Dorrit, father of the place. She is the central image of the cover design of the serial parts, caught in light made stronger by the prison's darkness, as she is seen too by Clennam entering the prison at the end of chapter 9. But Amy is no *alter ego* for Dickens, as David Copperfield was.

Dickens's depiction of the prison is undoubtedly drawn from his personal historical knowledge of it; the representation, though, is purged of personal reminiscence. In detail of its physical and social dispositions, it is remarkably accurate. What is 'wrong' is either irrelevant or the natural result of a child's limited understanding: – if Mr Dorrit entered the prison in 1805, then he would have been transferred to its new building (the Marshalsea of the novel) in 1811, while the 'revenue' offenders (p. 97) were royal navy prisoners sentenced by the Admiralty Court: their being allowed to mingle with the debtors except when someone came from some Office surely combines acute observation with enforcement of the novel's general satire. Yet even in this historical account of the Marshalsea, Dickens scarcely makes the prison seem remote or strange. True, it 'is gone now, and the world is none the worse without it' (p. 97), and Dickens has an account in the Preface (published in the serial's final double number), of his mild

4 See, e.g., my 'The Mythic Sorrows of Charles Dickens', *Literature and History*, I (1975), pp. 49–60 and especially pp. 55–6.

surprise at visiting the site and finding the main building still there, as it was until destroyed by fire in the early 1970s. After the opening declaration of its being gone, there is no other until the Preface. The emphasis, rather, is on the Marshalsea's abiding presence, its shadow and its taint, that makes so unreal for Little Dorrit the world of Italy. As part of the novel's metaphor of insolvency, the prison permeates the fabric and stands after Merdle has succumbed to pressure and the Clennam house fallen, its name resounding still in the final paragraphs even as Amy and Clennam pass down into the stream of time. The Marshalsea, so much part of Dickens's history and of his past, nonetheless seems foregrounded as part of the novel's realization of an abiding present, and it is to the nature of that present that in due course I want to return.

Accepting the novel's public contemporaneity, even though resistance to anachronism keeps Dickens to a high level of generality in his reference, and accepting the relationship of Dickens's personal history, of the 1850s and the 1820s, to the novel's concerns and materials, questions can still usefully be pursued about the degree and nature of historical representation in *Little Dorrit*. Set thirty years ago, what sense of history does the novel have? How far does Dickens seek, for instance, to give an historical dimension by detail or allusion? How too does he treat time, which is history's peculiar dimension?

Certainly, if we look first at the authenticating detail of the past, there is no antiquarianism nor does Dickens fall into obvious anachronisms: there are no trains, going to France (p. 715), if a suspiciously well-established steam crossing of the Channel (pp. 876, 878), while those were Diligence days (p. 876). Letters are refused at the door (p.380), presumably not only because Miss Wade is incommunicado, but because they are ante-1840 and not prepaid, while Mr Merdle's three rotten boroughs (pp. 619–20) need no enforcing reference of 'those days' or 'since swept away' to be pre-1832, though they gain a curiously current air as 'little rotten boroughs in this Island', where 'this' takes on its force of something 'close at hand' or 'familiar'. Occasionally Dickens emphasizes the past, by distancing references: no such place now stands where Casby's house stood (p. 185). This same sense of difference seems to underlie a contrast elaborated between the Adelphi terrace, overlooking the Thames, with the area thirty years ago:

> there being no small steam-boats on the river, no landing places but slippery wooden stairs and foot-causeways, no railroad on the oppo-

site bank, no hanging bridge or fish-market near at hand, no traffic on the nearest bridge of stone. (p. 586)

Such detail is, though, curiously personal for it had been on this Terrace in 1824 that the young Dickens, eating outside the Fox-under-the-hill, had watched some coal heavers dancing:[5] the scene was reproduced in *David Copperfield* (chapter 11) and we may see the Adelphi in *Little Dorrit* as not only a secluded spot where Clennam can observe Miss Wade and Rigaud but also a window back into Dickens's own history, even while it underlines the technical change and urban development of thirty years. Yet if it is personal, it is also very local in its intensity.

If such historical details offer the enforcing perspective of difference that makes history, they are not many in number and seem sometimes casual indeed: John Chivery's chaste neckerchief of a style 'much in vogue at that day' (p. 258) is a touch of ridicule rather than historical picturing; while the introduction of Old Nandy (p. 413) gives an utterly ahistorical coat worn by a man constantly with us. The more the novel is examined, indeed, the more a certain kind of detail of the past seems absent and the more also there seems to be a special use of details or of time to authenticate the narrative, while not rendering it remote or alien. The past that is different: – in social codes; in the controlling determinism of events; and in its influence upon fictive characters and their action; – can be rendered variously and not least by significant material detail of the kind (travel; dress; food; manners) already considered. That minutiae of a larger world that intermingles with the inner fictional world is curiously absent in *Little Dorrit*. At the level of the state and of political institutions, the king's name is never mentioned, nor his power invoked; while the Barnacles and Stiltstalkings are not made distinct from the office-holders of this latter day. Social details are taken for granted, not emphasized: the unhistorical nature of dress in the novel is reinforced by the mid-century costume, for ladies especially, in Phiz's illustrations. Dickens avoids gross anachronisms and indeed enforces certain differences between then and now in, for example, travel, the postal system, and rotten boroughs, despite which it is the sense of the present which predominates. Two examples, authenticating respectively Meagles and Doyce, may serve to suggest just how untied the action in fact is to a

5 John Forster, *The Life of Charles Dickens*, ed. J. W. T. Ley (London, 1928), p. 31.

pattern of those larger external events usual in historical novels. The examples serve also to suggest how Dickens in *Little Dorrit* is treating the past in a particular kind of way: first, how the reader is not disturbed by the difference of the past; second, how the novel's 'history' is internally self-consistent and independent of external 'big' histories. Meagles, in his strange chauvinistic way, has picked up two words of French, characteristic enough: more than once he refers to these foreigners' habit of 'allonging and marshonging', an allusion appropriately stereotypical and more delicate, from Dickens himself, than, say, 'Johnny Crapaud'. Yet while in the 1850s, despite Napoleon III's ban, the Marseillaise was no doubt typically French for Englishmen, revived as it had been at the 1830 revolution,[6] in the England of the 1820s, cut off from France by war and then from the anthem itself by the restored Bourbons, it is hardly likely to have been familiar or characteristic. To have found a more historically accurate equivalent of Frenchness would not necessarily have established Meagles so clearly: it stands, an unobtrusive anachronism, because of the historical and cultural insight it focuses through the present familiarity of the reader, which he feels to be appropriate, not strange. France offers, too, a potentially jarring or disruptive element of the historical surface if we scrutinise the story of the engineer, Doyce. His history is exemplary in its quiet usefulness and in Doyce's persistence against indifference and contempt in his own country: the barbaric Power 'with valuable possessions on the map of the world' (p. 735), later in his story, is clearly and ironically intended for Russia, the enemy of the 1850s which yet recognizes worth. Doyce's history needs time into which to expand backwards from 1826. Without being too pedantic, Doyce has by then been established in England for a good dozen years since his European travels (p. 233), which included Lyons, Germany, and St Petersburg. The dozen years take us back to 1814; and while a British citizen might be in Germany or Russia before then, it is hard to credit that he could be in the France of Napoleon. In making Doyce's history, Dickens has elided the Continental wars that figure so much in historical writings and in the nineteenth-century literary imagination.

And yet this exclusion is not simply because Dickens has flung in a little historical colouring and taken no notice of the narrative's chronology. The novel's main action, set over 1825–1826–1827, roughly corresponds to the timespan of writing and publication (from early

6 For the reappearance of the Marseillaise in 1830, see, e.g., Hector Berlioz, *Memoirs*, trans. David Cairns (London, 1969), pp. 131–4.

Spring 1855 to June 1857) and so the reading experience corresponds to the span of the main narrative. The entry of Dorrit into the Marshalsea, the birth of Amy in 1804, the absence of Clennam from England – this and all the internal chronology of the novel is carefully worked out and maintained.

All this, taken with the case of Meagles and the history of Doyce, suggests that Dickens is creating in *Little Dorrit* a world which does not exclude history, whether viewed from its situation in time (it is set thirty years back) or from its extension in time (it is chronologically self-consistent), but, almost as though he were writing a parallel or alternative history, Dickens leeches out what would distract from the contemporaneity, the public history, and presents a world innocent of external history (though innocent in that respect only). The French Revolution and the Napoleonic Wars are history; the Regency and the accession of George IV are history; the Luddite unrest and the agitation for Parliamentary reform are history. In historical fiction such events are acknowledged and used, in *Vanity Fair*, in *Shirley*, in *Middlemarch*. The fictive events are overlaid by the larger historical template. What *Little Dorrit* seems to emphasize (the result of a deliberate rather than a casual process), indifferent to these large events or even to the accidentals of the past, is an intensely consistent history of ordinary people, held steadily in time and unaffected by the articulation of great events.

History in *Little Dorrit* is the time of its action and the time of its characters, which works on the same time-scale as that of common human experience, but does not seek validation from an external and pre-existent public history. In a novel where the plot (however involved and unsatisfactory its resolution) turns on the initials 'DNF' ('Do Not Forget') imprisoned within a watch, time cannot be unimportant. History is the time of our lives (ticked out by the watch); and is the story of our lives (preserved by memory, by not forgetting); and is the interpretation of that story (Clennam and his father and Mrs Clennam all understand the initials differently). What treatment of time and what version of history does *Little Dorrit* offer? I want now to consider time and tense in the novel; and then time and character; before briefly viewing Amy as a figure in the landscape of Italy.

The idea of the past is emphatic in the novel's opening ('Thirty years ago') and in the roving back twenty years more to begin Dorrit's story: yet a continuum is established even in that opening by the blazing sun being 'no greater rarity in southern France then, than at any other time, before or since' (p. 39). The ordinariness of this experience, rather than its exceptional (because historical) nature is noted. And if 'before or since' is a Janus-expression, so too time in the novel works both ways. It goes back thirty years and again twenty years more, and by inference, further yet for Mr Dorrit's early life and Clennam's birth and his parents' history, even while it comes forward through a passing reference to Bar, his master-stroke remembered long after he gets made Attorney General (p. 617), a break into the narrative's future, unusual away from the perspectives of closure. Indeed, time comes to the present of writing (Clennam and Amy might still be alive when the novel was published), while John Chivery's 'tombstone' (p. 256) projects the contemporary reader into a remote future, of 1886, another thirty years, but now beyond the novel's writing. Twice more, with temporal variation, John Chivery's tombstone is mentioned (pp. 264, 802), its inscriptions underscoring the continuity and extension of time.

In a novel ostensibly of the past, time as present tense acquires a peculiar emphasis. It may only be in a rhetorical heightening, as when 'it may be long before this present narrative descries' release for Affery from her haunted state of mind (p. 229) or when words unspoken by Mr Dorrit are supplied for him (p. 526). It is more germane to the novel's themes in the 'magnates' that 'keep us going' (p. 294), while as Little Dorrit recalls the children huddled at night in the arcades of Covent Garden, hunted about like young rats, the narrator breaks through to present meaning in these same outcasts: 'look to the rats young and old, all ye Barnacles, for before God they are eating away our foundations, and will bring the roofs on our heads!' (p. 208). The military rats of the Italian barracks, too, 'were (happily) eating away the props of the edefices . . . and must soon, with them, be smashed' on the heads of soldiers, priests, and spies in the street below (p. 519): in 1826 the smash might be 1848, but in 1856 it may look forward also to 1860. Continuity rather than completion is suggested. The visions of these latter days, if with comic lights, foreshadow an end to things: the props to the Clennam house, gymnasium for neighbouring cats, are yet no very sure reliance (p. 71), and foreshadow the end of house and of Rigaud, as that fulfilment, planned from the beginning as Dickens was at pains to stress, is a metonymic accomplishment of that warning to the Barnacles and to ourselves in those Covent Garden Rats. Past in *Little Dorrit* is constantly being raised to the intensity of present, both because of the novel's contemporary themes and because of an individual continuity in its flow between thirty years ago and now.

This sense of the present is necessarily largely an effect wrought by the narrator. The narrative, though, is aware of how time, measured by the watch, affects people, and how for them the clock-time of experience is mingled with memory. If Amy, for all her twenty-two years, has the physical form of a child, she is what her history has made her, not what her body suggests, and a true reader of her face and her eyes sees how that history is written there, as Clennam, like the prostitute on Amy's 'party' night (pp. 217–18), recognizes that Amy is an adult with a knowledge beyond that of her real age. If Clennam, at forty, his life wasted as he believes, seems to have no history (his life in China is a blank, for all Flora's attempts comically to chronicle it), the gap represents partly the destructive effect of his upbringing, partly the way Mrs Clennam has sought to expunge the past, even while 'DNF' reaches across it, so that Arthur's nagging if wrongly directed enquiries finally bridge that gap and compel his mother to admit the truth of history. For Mrs Clennam has sought to arrest time: she asks abruptly, to Arthur's astonishment (it is only September), whether it is snowing outside (p. 74) and seems incapable, from her spatial location, where a fire burns throughout the year, the outside world excluded, of grasping change. Yet once history is resprung through the codicil that she has tried to keep buried, she is impelled by the consequences of time and of her own history to come to life, like that past, buried but never truly dead, and make her dash through the streets. Even the dead can have histories, whether it is the obscure life of Arthur's mother (fairly impenetrable even after the plot revelations) or that of Lillie Meagles, Pet's dead twin sister. Her life is mirrored in her sister's, as she is imagined growing along with Pet, and when Pet confirms that she is engaged to Henry Gowan, her sister too in a sense is engaged and then dies. Meagles says to Clennam, 'I feel . . . as if you had loved my dead child very tenderly, and had lost her when she was like what Pet is now' (p. 387). There is an Orphic echo here, of the dead being given and snatched away, though it is a garland of roses, not Clennam's (or anybody's) head that the river floats away that night.

Once out of the Marshalsea and in Italy, we reach a place full of history, or rather, one whose history has apparently ceased, except in the apocalyptic prospect of destruction. As the Dorrits approach Rome, the landscape degenerates, spatially rather than temporally, the scenes progressively 'growing more dirty and more haggard' (p. 566), and in Rome ruin and stagnation are the only principles, in a city 'where everything seemed to be trying to stand still for ever on the ruins of something else.' 'Trying to' undermines the striving for stasis and asserts the claims of time, as they are asserted against Mrs

Clennam, yet while Italy awaits its threatened future, there is no public present history of Doges or Popes or Austrians (are the soldiers in their barracks (p. 519) Italians or Austrians? their identity is stripped away). The history is remote and meaningless, so that for Amy this is a world of dream. Displaced suddenly from the only reality of the Marshalsea that has so deeply and intensely formed and imbued her, she suffers an emotional and mental paraplegia, her temporal dislocation mirrored in an unreal Italy. It is through her consciousness that much of this landscape is mediated either directly in her letters or at crucial moments by a narrator who draws us to her point of view. Ancient as these places are, they were there, in ruins, all the Marshalsea time (p. 609), which usurps upon them and enforces through Amy, her present temporal activity effectively suspended, how these are both places of insolvency: 'Two ruined spheres of action and suffering were before the solitary girl often sitting on some broken fragment' (p. 671).

Amy, Little Dorrit herself, of all the characters, has surely the most pronounced history – not the 'big' history of kings or nations, but the primary fictive history of Child of the Marshalsea ('My daughter; born here'). This is enforced by the pattern of the registers in St George's church, where she sleeps on her 'party' night: her birth is registered in one, she has 'Deaths' as her pillow that night, and she ends, in a notable disjunction of normal human history ('hatch, match, and despatch'), by completing the triplet with her marriage to Clennam. Through the technique of a dreamlike unreality her history seems suspended in Italy, even while, seeing Rome and recalling the Marshalsea, her inability to perceive them as other than ruins, stresses that history of hers and prepares us for her return to the stream of human temporal activity when her father lapses finally into the Marshalsea again. Amy, seated amidst the wreck of Rome's history, cannot shore these fragments against her ruin. Only when she is recalled to the present can she act and renew her history in the flowing continuum of time.

How then are history and time treated in *Little Dorrit*? First, there need be no doubt of the novel's contemporary purpose and hence of its contemporaneity; nor need there be any doubt of how in it can be traced something of Dickens's personal history of the 1850s and of the 1820s. Yet there are other forms of history too. In *Little Dorrit*, history, like the sun that shone on Marseilles thirty years ago, is both of those days (in the past) and yet extends onwards and backwards, to the present (the narrative's future) and to the deeper past. This stream of time which is the novel's history is that known also to us the readers, of which we are part, just as Doyce's story, not in any true sense anachronistic, is 'the matter-of-fact narrative which we all know by heart' (p. 161). That may be no more than a gesture towards the old truism of an unchanging human nature. Yet, more importantly, Dickens is representing, in Amy's intensity of time present and of dislocated history, in Doyce's familiar narrative, the continuousness of modern time which is the history of us all (beginning with self-consciousness), when, looking back, we sense a continuity of life, feeling no different now from what we were *then*. Our own lifetime is the present and as Amy and Clennam pass at the end into the roaring streets (p. 895), their time, however compressed in closure, is our time too, where we are jostled by the noisy and eager, by the arrogant, the froward, and the vain, or are (God save the mark!) those very makers of the 'usual uproar'.

Little Dorrit, for all that it eschews the 'big' histories, is deeply and constantly aware of time; its 'historical' personages are ordinary people, so that the novel presents a history of society and individuals, perceived not as events of a world-shaking kind, but as a constant unfolding of the ordinary. If our concept of history is the strange, the different, as it was for most historical novels, where the sense of distance is emphasized by disjunction of time, and reiterated by the romance of costumes, manners, speech, actions, a heightening and a colour, then in *Little Dorrit* we have a novel hardly touched by a sense of history, a novel in which Dickens essentially convinces us of a past which is familiar, the same. Only when time is broken are we aware of difference: as in the artificial freezing of pictures or photographs ('Did I wear those clothes?') or objects of the past ('How did they get their feet into shoes that size?') or behind long unopened doors. Occasionally, as I have suggested, Dickens dutifully includes that alien past through such brief momentary breaks (though when he wrote he was reminding many of his readers, as he reminded himself, of things not really alien because known in their own lifetime), of Diligences, of the steamer-free Thames, of cravats, of places now gone. True, the novel has a stronger sense of a different history, of a Covent Garden 'with famous coffee-houses, where gentlemen wearing gold-laced coats and swords had quarrelled and fought duels' (p. 208), of the 'good old days' (p. 73) of the state execution, a world of the Wisdom of Our Ancestors – of the block, the rack, the plague, as Dickens's joke false bookbacks in his library proclaimed it. That history is of a world beyond 1800 or 1789 and belongs only with the detritus of Meagles's souvenirs of his travels, the things that pass for history and truth, a world of the imagination in its way, but false to fact and to imagination, as Meagles's proudly displayed sticky saints on their baked blackness are false to art, as Dorrit's conception of vassalage towards Old Nandy is false. It is history as the ruins of Rome are history: remote, totally alien, not forming or part of the modern world.

Little Dorrit has a strong sense of history, because it has a strong sense of time. This time is the unbroken stream of our own lives, unaffected, as most of us feel our lives to be unaffected by an external or different historical texture, appropriate to a novel that demands we analyze and change the present state of things. Hence, it is a history that has meaning, not as the false imagination would trick it out with wigs and powder and duels and codes of honour, nor as antiquarians would turn it, explaining Bleeding Heart Yard, back into the dust to which the distant past has sunk, but meaning that links it seamlessly to the present of the narrative and of the reader. *Little Dorrit* may seem a novel scarcely historical, if we look for the history of *Ivanhoe* or *Henry Esmond* or *Westward Ho!* or *Romola* (and I name none of these novels slightingly); yet read as the history of a lifetime that stretches between its own time and thirty years ago, it is deeply and inherently of history and about history.

Space, Time, and Paradox: The Sense of History in Hardy's Last Novels

TERENCE WRIGHT

We'll close up Time, as a bird its van,
We'll traverse Space, as spirits can. (*The Dynasts*)

Hardy's last and greatest fiction lies between the two works which are most self-consciously 'historical' in his *oeuvre* – *The Trumpet Major* and *The Dynasts*. Both deal with the period of the Napoleonic Wars, and both technically attempt to distance the reader from events. *The Trumpet Major* is like a fly in amber, a vignette of events now long gone. Past, present, and future are all contained in it, but the novel's 'future' is 'now' for the reader. It is this which gives the elegiac note characteristic of the work, and also the tempering irony implicit in the hopes, desires, loves, and sacrifices of so many hearts now turned to dust. The 'staying power' of objects – the mill, the landscape, the grass walk in the garden ever to be gravelled – bears witness to the comparative mutability of mankind. The concept of 'big' history – that is, major public, largely political, events – also emphasises the contrast with the history of individual lives. When Anne watches the King on the Esplanade, she

> now felt herself close to and looking into the stream of recorded history, within whose banks the littlest things are great, and outside which she and the general bulk of the human race were content to live on as an unreckoned, unheeded superfluity. (p. 123)[1]

Above all, *The Trumpet Major* is haunted, for all its romantic comedy, by death. The 'ring' of John Loveday's 'smart step' into the night on the last page of the book '[dies] away' on the ears of his family, as the sight of them at the lighted doorway dies away for us. Like Keats's lovers, they are gone, 'ay, ages long ago'.

The Dynasts deliberately abstracts the movement of history on the

[1] All page references to Hardy's novels in the text are to the New Wessex edn, General Editor, P. N. Furbank (London, 1975–76).

large scale from the doings of individuals, in this way reiterating more starkly than *The Trumpet Major* the irony of history, and making explicit its unknowable quality. If the Spirits are a poetic, choric device, they also represent emotions and tendencies on a superhuman scale and lead to a sense of division running through the work as a whole – large and small, flesh and spirit. It is perhaps the very self-consciously historical cast of these works which leads me to focus rather on fictions which are superficially less relevant to Hardy's idea of history.

Both *The Trumpet Major* and *The Dynasts*, as I have said, encourage our sense of detachment. In both works we are encouraged to share a superior, god-status. We look at a picture, watch a drama. It is 'then', or 'there'. By contrast, works such as *The Return of the Native*, *The Mayor of Casterbridge*, *Tess of the D'Urbervilles*, and above all *Jude the Obscure* have a raw, contemporary quality. The 'now' does not remove us from history, but involves us painfully in it. This is not to imply that Hardy's view of history overall is radically different when he is writing of his own times. Irony, unknowableness, the smallness of Man compared to the largeness of his passions, and many other themes are to be found throughout Hardy's work. It is the attitude of the author which is different, the way in which he thinks of history, the weight he gives to individual 'histories', the emotions aroused in him (and by implication in us) by a consideration of what has made us how we are. Moreover, since he is, in his later fiction (with the partial exception of *The Mayor of Casterbridge*), writing novels which are not primarily historical, the sense of history arises more subtly, organically, and perhaps with greater complexity in these works.

Most notably Hardy captures with his greatest intensity in the last novels a truth found also in his overtly historical works, namely that history is both process and stasis, that it may be apprehended spatially as well as temporally. The concept is so crucial in Hardy because it is at the root of his 'poetic' sense of history. As a process history is a matter of time, operating linearly, traceable as cause and effect. But there is in the poet a constant inclination towards the compression of the image, opposing and expanding things in space. At its most banal, this would make history a passive thing 'then' – a self-enclosed, perhaps sentimental picture. We have seen that Hardy avoids this trap in *The Trumpet Major* by implying resonances beyond the world of 'then'. But in *Tess* and *Jude* the spatial confrontation involved in people meeting their past reveals devastatingly that history is as much 'now' as 'then'. In broader terms, the spatial aspect means that Hardy's vision constantly expands 'sideways' into images. Images of history are at the heart of my discussion, and for my first image I shall go back seven years before even *The Trumpet Major* was written – to an incident in *A Pair of Blue Eyes*.

Suspended on the terrible cliff-face, in imminent peril of death, unable to see whether Elfriede Swancourt has yet arrived bringing hope for his recovery, Henry Knight lies 'hand-in-hand with the world in its infancy. Not a blade, not an insect, which spoke of the present, was between him and the past' (p. 221). His eye alights upon an embedded fossil, and his gaze is returned by those eyes, 'dead and turned to stone' (p. 222). In a moment 'time [closes] up like a fan before him' and he sees the whole panorama of history from 'fierce men, clothed in the hides of beasts', to the iguanadon 'and so on, till the lifetime scenes of the fossil confronting him were a present and modern condition of things' (p. 223).

Here encapsulated in a few moments of an early novel is Hardy's mature view of history, terrible in its indifference, human and yet inhuman. Spatial and temporal, individual and race, are brought together in a confrontation spanning aeons. The individual facing extinction, pitted against the 'inveterate antagonism' of earth – rock and stone –, mirrors the history of the race. The fossil reminds us that Darwin has lengthened and transformed our view of time, and that human history cannot now be separated from the story of all life, and indeed all things. Eye to eye, fossil and man speak of a 'progress' of history which amounts only to unimaginable antiquity and total insignificance.

More specifically, there are in this incident three major sub-divisions of history in Hardy's work, all carrying their own weight of significance. First is 'object history' – the rocky cliff, and buried within it the dead-alive fossil. Second is 'race history', the development of man out of lower forms, with the attendant questions of the direction and meaning of this development. Finally we have 'personal history', a concept which is more than a play on words. Hardy frequently speaks of his characters' 'history' and, as we shall see, it involves generally a placing of the self in relation to object and race history. Knight's minutes on the cliff-face, suspended in time, circumscribed in space, are analogous in individual terms to the supposed flash of the drowning man's whole life before him, but Knight has leisure to see beyond his own years to the ages of cause and effect, mutation and development, that have brought him to this lonely death. Typically, human nature refuses to accept the place assigned to it by history. Knight, faced with his own and his whole race's insignificance, nevertheless asserts the will to live:

> He dared not move an inch. Was Death really stretching out his hand? The previous sensation, that it was improbable he would die, was fainter now.
>
> However, Knight still clung to the cliff. (p. 223)

'Survival of the fittest' is a concept cruelly proposed to Knight, not as an idea in a book, but as a personal challenge for twenty minutes of his life. The reiterated image of grasping hands, it might be noticed, equates our origins with death. The most powerful connection we have with history is the inescapableness of our own demise.

On this occasion Knight escapes. He clings on to be rescued by Elfriede, but his symbolic freedom is not generally to be found in Hardy's later fiction. It is the fate of many of Hardy's major figures to be the victims of history. Personal history, however, can only be understood in the context of the other two categories, 'object' and 'race' history, which I have postulated, and in truth all three shape each other and appear as complex images which to some extent we 'murder to dissect'. Bearing all this in mind, I shall try to capture all three categories 'on the wing' as it were, by developing the history of individuals through the spatial sense of objects and the linear sense of our racial heritage.

In considering the individual destinies of Hardy's major protagonists, Tess Durbeyfield must instantly attract our attention as a woman whose personal history is manifestly related to some idea of 'history'. 'Is she a young woman whose history will bear investigation?' Mrs Clare asks her son (p. 289), with unconscious irony. Tess's d'Urberville past illustrates the immediacy of that 'spatial' poetic sense of history of which I spoke earlier. The connection between then and now may be traced rationally, linearly – as a decline, or a circle, for example, but most powerfully Tess is a child of the past when she is placed against it with the immediacy of an image. Hardy is unconcerned with tracing the socio-economic changes from mediaeval to nineteenth-century life. His commentary gets no further than ironic *exposés* of the impenetrability of historic process. But when Clare remarks on her likeness to her ancestors, and she looks into the eyes of their portraits, we feel a terrible confrontation with the inescapable past – that 'real history' which, said A. N. Whitehead, 'does not get written, because it is not in people's brains but in their nerves and vitals.' The point is made again in Jude's aunt's insistence that marriage has always been bad for the Fawleys. Is this to be interpreted as a matter of temperament? A curse? A product of the old lady's crusty temperament? It is never explained in these empirical terms or any others, but its inexplicable nature works as a resonant image of the past bequeathing an inheritance which is with us now and, *via* our choices, shapes our future. The inexplicable nature of the images is important, since, as I have remarked, history for Hardy is as inscrutable as the stone images of the d'Urberville knights and dames who sleep on 'unknowing'. As we shall see, stones are among the most important features of Hardy's 'object history'.

The spatial dimension is felt in *Tess* as an aspect of life's pilgrimage (through a landscape as well as through time) and on various specific occasions as a parallel or an adjunct to a temporal image. As Tess is lost in reverie, driving her cart through the dark lanes, 'the occasional heave of the wind became the sigh of some immense sad soul, conterminous with the universe in space, and with history in time' (p. 56). And so she falls to examining the 'mesh of events in her own life', until she loses all sense of time and place, only to be woken by the disastrous collision with the mail-cart. Ironically, in reviewing the tangled mesh of cause and effect in her personal history, she has lost connection quite literally with time and space, until those urgent arbiters of human affairs bring her to a terrible sense of reality – the 'mesh' of historical circumstance which is to trap her. Tess is an intelligent, and a moderately well-educated girl. Unlike her mother, whose idea of the evolution of things is confined to single days, Tess has an idea of history, which she confides to Clare:

> '. . . what's the use of learning that I am one of a long row only – finding out that there is set down in some old book somebody just like me, and to know that I shall only act her part; making me sad, that's all. The best is not to remember that your nature and your past doings have been just like thousands' and thousands', and that your coming life and doings'll be like thousands' and thousands'.' (pp. 153–4)

Tess longs to escape from this linear progression of days. Her longing is a more extreme and intense development of Eustacia Vye's. Eustacia, with her spyglass and hourglass, symbolizing respectively her desire for a wider horizon and the imprisonment in time which is marked by the running sands, looks to a fantasy of continental city life. Tess looks beyond life itself. She wishes for marriage with Clare, but there is a transcendent defeatism in her nature which looks for suspension of time and a proscribing of space. So she wishes that she and Clare could court forever, tells of how the soul may escape the body by fixing one's mind upon a star, and enjoys her few days of happiness with her husband in the empty house, unconscious of time and preserved from movement. The numerous references to Eden suggest the state before history had begun, and the life of her baby reduces all time and space to insignificant solipsism:

> a waif to whom eternal Time had been a matter of days merely, who knew not that such things as years and centuries ever were; to whom the cottage interior was the universe, the week's weather climate, new-born babyhood human existence, and the instinct to suck human knowledge. (p. 124)

There is in Tess's relationship to history a certain paradox. The more she understands of the meaning of history, the less meaning it has for her. Her parents and her lover rush to connect her with the d'Urbervilles. She flees the baleful idea. In *Jude the Obscure* the paradoxes are more striking and varied. If this is the most contemporary, indeed the most forward-looking, of Hardy's works, it is also the one in which we are most painfully reminded of the past. The world of *Jude* is one of rapid communication. Letters are constantly sent back and forth, warning, delaying, anticipating. Railway is the almost universal form of transport. Sue declares that she would rather sit in the railway station than a Cathedral: 'That's the centre of the town life now. The Cathedral has had its day!' (p. 154). For Tess it is a matter of wonder that the train will take milk to people in London who know nothing of her doings, but Jude and Sue travel constantly and rapidly by train, their lives dominated by the necessity of remembering departure times. Sue is surprised that 'such a powerful organization as a railway-train should be brought to a standstill on purpose for her' (p. 252). So dominant is the railway that Hardy can speak of Jude '[timing Sue] by the only possible train'. *The Return of the Native*, *The Mayor of Casterbridge*, *Tess*, are pedestrian tragedies, but *Jude* is a railway tragedy, this swift, punctual, wide-reaching mode of transport imaging as well as making possible what Hardy dubs the 'modern vice of unrest' (p. 108). Yet for all this the movement of the novel is not one of progress, but rather of regression. *Jude* is also an urban tragedy. The railway runs between towns in which Jude and Sue find work and lodgings, but a change of place does not mean an advance, any more than a passage of time. Jude sets his gaze towards the 'heavenly Jerusalem', not recognizing that mankind is already in the city, and it is far from celestial. He becomes a skilled stonemason, but eventually is reduced to rough work for poor cottagers, while the fatal attraction of Christminster decides the place of his death, abandoned and excluded. Phillotson advances to Christminster only to return finally to Marygreen. Even the practical Arabella is defeated by emigration and returns from Australia to her old haunts. Disastrous human relationships of the past are established again in the re-marriages of the four main protagonists. Psychologically, Sue regresses to a primitive state on the death of her children, a movement which has, as we shall see, wider implications than the fate of a single person.

Early in his career Jude carves on the back of a milestone an arrow pointing to Christminister, and beneath it the word 'THITHER'. He symbolizes thereby not only his own aspirations but a general faith in progress, a goal to which we are striving, and at which we must ultimately arrive. This, as we have seen, is at variance with the general movement of human affairs in the novel, which is regressive and circular. This stone is also one instance of the things on which we leave our imprint. Before the book is ended the carving is already obscured by moss. So it is with all the works of man. 'Object history' is in fact evidence of human history, but all that such evidence shows is our own impermanence. The stone mouldings of Christminster are 'wounded, broken, sloughing off their outer shape in the deadly struggle against years, weather, and man' (p. 107). The Roman road is 'neglected and overgrown'. The field in which Jude is set to scare birds is covered by fresh harrow lines,

> lending a meanly utilitarian air to the expanse, taking away its gradations, and depriving it of all history beyond that of the few recent months, though to every clod and stone there really attached associations enough and to spare – echoes of songs from ancient harvest-days, of spoken words, and of sturdy deeds. (p. 38)

Yet beneath these temporary deformations the rock from which the stone is quarried, the land which yields the harvests, remains intact. Man is like the painting of the 'Three Mariners' on the signboard in *The Mayor of Casterbridge*, forming after the ravages of time 'but a half-invisible film upon the reality of the grain, and knots, and nails, which composed the signboard' (p. 72). The personal history of Jude is a manifestation of man's relation to objects. Initially he is in love with 'history' in the shape of the 'dead' languages and the rotten stones of Christminster, and in hope of the future. Yet personal experience shows him the falsity of this position. It is not long before he realizes that the main street of Christminster 'had more history than the oldest college in the city' (p. 139). The paradox is captured in Jude's chosen trade of stone-masonry. Renovation of the ancient and decayed stone-work provides him with a practical means of livelihood, and also allows him to participate in an 'effort as worthy as that dignified by the name of scholarly study within the noblest of the colleges' (p. 108). Yet he is also, as in his scholarly studies, merely propping up 'medi-aevalism' which was 'as dead as a fern-leaf in a lump of coal' (p. 108). What Jude is made, perforce, to realize, is that the 'here and now' is a manifestation of a truer history than mediaevalism. This truer history 'short circuits' us to our more primitive selves – manifested in *The Return of the Native* as paganism. Isolated upon Egdon Heath, 'homage to nature', 'fragments of Teutonic rites', 'seem in some way or other to have survived mediaeval doctrine' (p. 385). At Shaston, Stoke-Bare-hills, and Christminster, in *Jude*, the modern and the historic stand side by side, but ancient and modern are one in being reduced to scratches on the surface of an oblivious pre-history.

The stony earth itself is a central paradox for Hardy. Mute, immutable, it yet speaks of man, but only to bear witness to his mutability. The fossil outstares Knight with its truth; Stonehenge, raised by man, is indifferent to him; the tombs of the d'Urbervilles outlast their tenants' flesh and bones. The cusped and phallic stones at Flintcomb-Ash mock the futile attempts at cultivation imposed upon them.

Man and object are connected by other images than stone. 'Face', for example, is an interchangeable epithet between human and landscape. Egdon Heath is a 'face on which time makes but little impression'. Clym Yeobright is seen in the landscape like 'a fly on the face of a negro'. In *Tess* the sky and earth at Flintcomb-Ash are two visages confronting each other. And in sleep, by a reverse process, we are told in *The Mayor of Casterbridge*, 'there come to the surface buried genealogical facts' (p. 147). Before she sees Alec for the first time, Tess

> had dreamed of an aged and dignified face, the sublimation of all the d'Urberville lineaments, furrowed with incarnate memories representing in hieroglyphic the centuries of her family's and England's history. (p. 64)

Reinforced in all these instances is the interrelation between personal history – experience – and the way 'things' are ('things' ambiguously referring to the laws of nature which make history, and to the objects in which history is made manifest). Yet it demonstrates the artificiality of any piecemeal dissection of Hardy's sense of history that the face of the individual is probably most significant for showing us 'race history'. This is certainly true of the most famous discussion of a face in his work, at the beginning of Book III of *The Return of the Native*: 'In Clym Yeobright's face could be dimly seen the typical countenance of the future' (p. 185). The passage is too well-known to need exposition here, its main purport being summarized in the phrase 'the age of a modern man is to be measured by the intensity of his history' (p. 156), but the word 'future' suggests the yet more sombre and terminal view of the race found in the octogenarian face of 'Little Father Time'. The fact that the type in *Jude* is represented by a child suggests the reductiveness of Hardy's vision. We may say of Clym that personal experiences have left their mark upon his face. His disillusionment with Paris, and subsequently his tragic involvement with two women, comprise a personal history which reveals in his countenance a tragic race history as perceived by himself. But Little Father Time has no perceived personal history. He has been born with direct race-knowledge, arriving out of the paradoxical 'new' world of Australia. He returns to the old world equipped with a knowledge he need never have travelled to obtain. The child, leaving the station, falls into a 'steady mechanical creep' (p. 291). The words are suggestive not merely because 'creeping' is uncharacteristic of an eight-year-old child, but because symbolically it is the movement history assumes for the last decade of the nineteenth century. It is the stealthy, inevitable tread of a 'progress' which is not progress. In place of the 'march' of time, ushering in a new age, we have the creep of a tired child arriving unexpectedly by night – evolution overtaking us with race exhaustion and death. Little Father Time embodies one of Hardy's bleakest insights into history, namely that not only is history most apparent in the 'now', but that it also contains our future. Sue feels that 'we have returned to Greek joyousness, and have blinded ourselves to sickness and sorrow, and have forgotten what twenty-five centuries have taught the race since their time' (p. 309).

Jude foresees the death of man in only fifty or a hundred years. Ultimately he has learned that 'history' is all life, whenever it is being lived – the eternal 'now' gathering up the past and shaping the future. A common movement pervades object, race, and person, binding them all to a history before memory, even before consciousness, approximated by the landscape, with its reminders of the antiquity of man, his kinship with the earth, the rudimentary nature of his artefacts, in the shape of barrows, flints, and stone monuments. All declare that we share the fate of earth. This is our true 'history'. It is a cliché of the theory of history that we may learn lessons from the study of our past, but those characters in Hardy's fiction who exemplify this truth learn something which is life-negating and destructive for them personally. Tess wishes for escape in transcendence, Jude dies in the bitter recognition of futility. Sue Bridehead is most significant of all. In her, knowledge of the arbitrary primitiveness of history is matched by a return to a psychological primitiveness. Paradoxically the sophistication of intellectual awareness manifests itself in her as an anthropomorphising of 'the way things are' into a sentient enemy. Her self-flagellation in returning to Phillotson is an attempt to placate 'gods' who do not hear her, to interpret morally, as a lesson, an amoral state of things. This 'fetichism' (to use one of Hardy's more favoured words) contrasts with the pragmatism of those who do not see history as a lesson. Physician Vilbert, we are told when we first encounter him, is 'a survival', and indeed we see him flourishing still at the end of *Jude*, and even courting his fellow-survivor, Arabella Donn. The word 'survival' is a crucial one in a post-Darwinian age. The reddleman Diggory Venn in *The Return of the Native* is described as

> filling at present in the rural world the place which, during the last century, the dodo occupied in the world of animals. He is a curious, interesting, and nearly perished link between obsolete forms of life and those which generally prevail. (pp. 37–8)

The terminology, although half-facetiously metaphorical, hints at biological struggles for survival – 'extinct', 'the dodo', 'curious link', 'obsolete forms of life'. The final paradox would seem to be that 'survival of the fittest' may not mean survival of the most intellectually and emotionally advanced – that indeed these much-vaunted features of human superiority may be a hindrance in the long-run. Joan Durbeyfield shows the spirit of survival after Tess's marriage, taking her daughter's return 'as a thing which had come upon them irrespective of desert or folly; a chance external impingement to be borne with; not a lesson' (p. 282). The widow Edlin, in *Jude*, is similarly pragmatic in her strictures on marriage:

> 'Matrimony have growed to be that serious in these days that one really do feel afeard to move in it at all. In my time we took it more careless; and I don't know that we was any the worse for it!' (pp. 375–6)

Do we make history, or are we made by it? Hardy would seem to say that those who make it, by bringing to life the overview of a fully-developed consciousness, who see the interlocking of 'then' and 'now', and its implications for the future, are doomed to suffer, while the passive pragmatists 'made' by history are content with their lot. Whichever way it is taken, history for Hardy is deeply negative. Its negativity is part of a greatness of vision which understands history as an image of the human condition, seen at a painful juncture between two ages. On the one hand is the positive freshness of Romanticism. Contrast the octogenarian-faced Little Father Time with Wordsworth's children who 'sport upon the shore' of eternity, while the soul, travelling 'in a moment thither', gains joy from strength and security. Little Father Time's shore yields no such 'sporting' or sense of security:

> A ground swell from ancient years of night seemed now and then to lift the child in this his morning-life, when his face took a back view over some great Atlantic of Time, and appeared not to care about what it saw. (p. 289)

Again, where Wordsworth celebrates the careless particularity of the child mind, untrammelled by adult concepts of 'then and now', 'here and there' ('We are Seven', 'Anecdote for Fathers'), Little Father Time is preternaturally aware of the overview. His sense of history is already fully, and tragically, developed, as he sits 'passive and regarding his companions as if he saw their whole rounded lives rather than their immediate figures' (p. 290).

Again, we could look back to the way in which the Romantics saw objects. Keats's urn, for example, 'doth tease us out of thought as doth eternity'. Like Hardy's object it answers no questions, but its silent endurance is reassurance of a transcendent and comforting truth – 'a friend to man'. An even more direct contrast is to be found if we consider the stones of the uncompleted sheepfold in Wordsworth's *Michael*. Superficially the picture is the same as that projected by Hardy's stones. Stone endures, a symbol of man's fruitless struggle to transcend his own times and passions. Yet there are fundamental differences between the late Victorian and the Romantic vision. Not only does Wordsworth celebrate the 'comfort in the strength of love', but the stones of Michael's sheepfold speak positively to us. They are not indifferent, but partake, in the poet's rhetoric, of a history as cultured as it is ancient. The sheepfold is a covenant such as God made with Abraham. It is sanctified by religion, society, and tradition, and far from convincing us of the insignificance of our past, binds us to our Fathers through generations:

> '. . . let this Sheep-fold be
> Thy anchor and thy shield; amid all fear
> And all temptation, let it be to thee
> An emblem of the life thy Fathers liv'd,
> Who, being innocent, did for that cause
> Bestir them in good deeds.' (11.417–22)

All that is lost to Hardy, as it is lost to Jude, when he views the rotten stones of Christminster with the eye of experience. In the intervening century Earth has become a presence we no longer feel as a mother, solitude has become loneliness, awe at the wonder of creation has turned to despair at its indifference. To the science of Darwin has been added the pessimism of Schopenhauer. It is not that Hardy has abandoned Romanticism. He still 'reads' the rocks and stones; he still has a concept called 'nature'. These things are still for him 'presences'. But their message has changed.

By the same token Hardy is not a full-blown twentieth-century existentialist. The world does not disintegrate; even in its indifference it has a massive presence, like the unseen shapes of the columns of Stonehenge as Clare and Tess stand beneath them. Our history is contained in these presences, and even in this we are linked to things inextricably. Hardy's characters are not infected with the disgust and boredom we feel in *The Waste Land*, Sartre's *La Nausée*, the later Beckett, many parts of Lawrence. There is a clear-sighted confrontation of circumstance which keeps his heroes and heroines in the mould of an older tragic ideal. To this extent Hardy needs history itself as a metaphoric expression of his sense of negativity. Stephen Dedalus experiences at least the possibility of wakening from his 'nightmare of history'. Hardy's characters remain in it, defined by it, not cast away on a sea of disintegrating experience. Yet in Tess's vision of unending, meaningless days, in Jude's farcically futile attempt to drown himself in the frozen pond, and Sue's neurotic indecision as to what she is and what she wants, in her 'modern nerves', in every person's ultimate loneliness, we may feel the pangs of the twentieth century's alienation.

'History, All That': Revival Historiography and Literary Strategy in the 'Cyclops' Episode in *Ulysses*

ANDREW GIBSON

The centrality of Irish history as a theme in *Ulysses* has seldom been sufficiently emphasized. Yet Irish history is in part the nightmare from which it tries by various and sometimes profoundly subtle expedients to awake. Irish history is stamped indelibly on the core of the book from the start: from the situation with which we begin in the Martello tower, and from Stephen's darkly imaginative broodings on Irish history that dominate Joyce's 'Telemachiad' and are in fact its primary concern.[1] In one of its aspects, indeed, *Ulysses* may be read as a sustained and complex reflection on Irish history. History emerges repeatedly as a crucial if sometimes buried concern in episodes of the book where 'realist narrative' or 'styles' are what first engage our attention, from 'Aeolus' through 'Sirens' and 'The Oxen of the Sun' to 'Eumaeus'. In fact, the formal concerns in the later episodes are very often themselves an extension of and a reflection back on historical ones.

History is a theme in *Ulysses* both as record of the past and as discourse, and this is very much the case with the 'Cyclops' episode. From Kenner's *Dublin's Joyce* onwards, at least, scholars have recognized that 'Cyclops' develops a 'critique' of aspects of what have been described as the 'neo-Celtic movement' and its 'pseudo-histories'.[2] Relevant names have been named.[3] Yet this aspect of 'Cyclops' has

1 An excellent account of 'Telemachus', relevant here, is L. H. Platt, 'The Buckeen and the Dogsbody: Aspects of History and Culture in "Telemachus"', *James Joyce Quarterly*, 27 (1989), pp. 77–87.

2 Hugh Kenner, *Dublin's Joyce* (London, 1955), p. 255; Kenner, quoted in Karen Lawrence, *The Odyssey of Style in Ulysses* (Princeton, 1981), p. 101. Such terms effectively pass judgement from the start (this sort of material will not be worth a very serious consideration).

3 See, e.g., Kenner, pp. 191, 255; Phillip F. Herring (ed.), *Joyce's Notes and Early Drafts for Ulysses: Selections from the Buffalo Collection* (Charlottesville, 1977), pp. 134–5; C. H. Peake, *James Joyce: The Citizen and the Artist* (London, 1977), p. 237; and Daniel R. Schwarz, *Reading Joyce's Ulysses* (Basingstoke, 1987), pp. 177, 224.

usually been seen as of secondary importance alongside – on the one hand – the criticism it is commonly supposed to be developing of the Citizen, nationalism and political violence, and intolerance; and, on the other, the stout resistance Bloom puts up to the Citizen and his attitudes.[4] The point therefore needs to be made rather firmly: 'Cyclops' offers – amongst other things – a sustained assault on Revivalist historiographies and constructions of Irish history, and the aesthetics and politics implicit in them. The forms of historical imagination in question are those chiefly familiar from the work of Ferguson, O'Curry, Yeats, Lady Gregory, Douglas Hyde, and, above all, Standish O'Grady. The attack is central to the episode in a way that is seldom recognized. It serves as a context for the other themes in the episode, rather than a more or less incidental embroidery upon them. In this respect, it is worth reminding ourselves at once that Joyce's 'initial impulse' with 'Cyclops' was 'in the direction of the parody passages rather than in that of the first person naturalistic narrator' – or the naturalistic narrative – also present in the episode.[5] This may in itself provide some indication of how we might reassess our priorities as 'Cyclops' readers.

It was Samuel Ferguson, of course, who began to assert that, to consolidate their position in the unsettling wake of Catholic emancipation, the Anglo-Irish needed to unearth an authentically Irish past with which it might be possible to identify. It led him to forge an alliance with the scholars – Petrie, O'Curry, O'Donovan – who had already begun to salvage something of that ancient Irish culture. More importantly, it led him to translate an old Irish poetry that contained the legends and sagas of the pre-Christian, heroic age.[6] But if Ferguson insisted on the need for an Anglo-Irish accommodation with the Gaelic past, it was in O'Grady that that insistence flowered. The result of O'Grady's effort to put together the narrative of the Red Branch or Ulster Cycle is the most crucial work of Irish historiography of the period, the two volumes of the *History of Ireland* (1878–80). Its importance in the culture Joyce knew can hardly be underestimated.[7] It was enormously influential on Yeats, and on Lady Gregory, whose *Gods*

4 See, e.g., Michael Mason, *James Joyce: Ulysses* (London, 1972), p. 52; Patrick Parrinder, *James Joyce* (Cambridge, 1984), p. 172; and Schwarz, pp. 175–6.

5 Michael Groden, *Ulysses in Progress* (Princeton, 1977), p. 118.

6 F. S. L. Lyons, *Culture and Anarchy in Ireland 1890–1939* (Oxford, 1982), pp. 28–31.

7 Lyons, pp. 33–5.

and Fighting Men and *Cuchulain of Muirthemne*, for instance, sustain its mode of historical imagination. It had a similar influence on Hyde, as he turned to oral traditions preserved by the peasantry for what he took to be a dimension of history otherwise beyond the reach of the educated. Again and again, the emphasis is on history as retrieval, the 'disclosure' of an 'ancient tradition', as Lady Gregory put it, that is also a way of connecting up with that tradition.[8] Ferguson, for example, clearly saw himself as 'No rootless colonist of alien earth', but a man aspiring 'To link his present with his country's past/ And live anew in knowledge of his sires'.[9] The enterprise is in intention holistic, unifying. Part of O'Grady's purpose, for example, was clearly, as he said, 'to express the whole nature of a race or nation.'[10] History thus attempts to articulate the conscience of the race. Yet in point of fact the historiography in question was primarily an Anglo-Irish endeavour – in its formative stages, at least – and therefore, as is clear in Ferguson's original insistence, an appropriation of a past by those to whom it did not truly belong.

If Revivalist historiography of this kind is concerned with the ancient heroic past, it is also concerned with the relation between that past and the present and future. 'The gigantic conceptions of heroism and strength,' O'Grady wrote, 'with which the forefront of Irish history is thronged, prove the great future of this race and land' (*HCP*, p. 58). But in between the heroic past and the present and future, of course, there yawned a huge gap which made Revival history seem a good deal less than an 'expression' of a 'whole nature'. In particular, Revival histories minimized the place and importance of Ireland's Christian history and traditions.[11] For O'Grady, for example, the advent of Christianity had 'ruined' the ancient culture.[12] It had also 'ended the golden age of bardic composition' (*H*, II.24). Mediaeval

8 Lady Gregory, *The Kiltartan Poetry Book: Prose Translations from the Irish* (Dublin, 1918), p. vi.

9 Sir Samuel Ferguson, 'Mesgedra', in *Lays of the Red Branch* (Dublin, 1897), pp. 32–3.

10 Standish O'Grady, *History of Ireland: Critical and Philosophical* (Dublin, 1881), p. 5: references to this edition, in the text, by the abbreviation *HCP*. A. P. W. Malcomson describes the 'claim to speak on behalf of "the country" ' as characteristic of the Ascendancy class from the eighteenth century: quoted in Roy Foster, *Modern Ireland 1600–1972* (London, 1988), p. 173.

11 Cf. L. H. Platt, 'Joyce and the Anglo-Irish Revival: the Triestine Lectures', *James Joyce Quarterly* (forthcoming).

12 Standish O'Grady, *History of Ireland* (London, 1878–80), 2 vols, I.xv: references to this edition, in the text, by the abbreviation *H*.

Ireland in particular had been characterized by a 'rationalism and logic' which had been 'primarily responsible for the cloud which hangs over our early history' (*HCP*, p. 63). The middle ages themselves were little more than 'a scuffling of kites and crows' (*H*, II.34). So, too, for Lady Gregory, part of the excitement of reading Hyde's translations in *Love Songs of Connacht* was the sudden sense they provided of connection with a pre-mediaeval era and a tradition that 'existed in Ireland before Chaucer lived'.[13] For O'Grady, the 'scholastic Irish were great in annals and chronology, but the functions of the poet and maker were not theirs, nor vividness of perception, nor sympathy, nor grandeur of thought' (*HCP*, p. 166). The choice between Oisin and Patrick was clear. So was the choice between the heroic past and mediaeval and subsequent Catholic culture in Ireland. So, too, was the choice between ways of imagining history. O'Grady's establishes itself partly in ideal reaction to Catholic historiographers 'great in annals and chronology'.

It is a way of imagining history that blurs the borderlines between history and mythology, legend, folk-lore. The interest was – to quote Lady Gregory – in 'myth turned into history, or history into myth.'[14] One of the things that Lady Gregory herself clearly relished about oral tradition was that, far from preserving historical fact, it speedily dehistoricized the historical. O'Connell, for example, though dead for 'only sixty years', had 'already been given a miraculous birth, and the power of a saint' was 'on its way to him' (*KHB*, p. 51). O'Grady likewise rejected 'mere history', the 'merely archaeological' (*H*, II.17, *H*, I.iii). 'In history,' he writes in his introduction to the *History of Ireland*, 'there must be sympathy, imagination, creation' (*H*, I.iv). But he saw the exercise of the historical imagination as more than just individual. For 'century after century,' he wrote, the mind of Ireland 'was inflamed by the contemplation of . . . mighty beings' (*H*, I.vi). To O'Grady, his own historical imagination is an extension but also a reawakening of this mind, of a national historical imagination capable of returning to a people its own mythology. This is to be accomplished, however, not through 'the labours of the patient brood of scholars' but by a recasting of 'that old heroic history' in 'a literary form' (*H*, I.40). This, for O'Grady, is the only useful history, 'that kind of history which

13 Lady Gregory, *Poets and Dreamers: Studies and Translations from the Irish* (Dublin, 1903), p. 47.

14 Lady Gregory, *The Kiltartan History Book* (Dublin, 1909), p. 49: references to this edition, in the text, by the abbreviation *KHB*.

a nation desires to possess', one that represents 'the imagination of the country', betrays 'the ambition and ideals of the people', and thus has 'a value far beyond the tale of actual events and duly recorded deeds' (*H*, I.22).

It is thus a history that requires and creates heroic forms. It encourages and thrives on exaggeration, as Lady Gregory praises the legends of Finn because they are 'the most exaggerated of the tales' of the Fianna and therefore those 'most often in the mouths of the people' (*KHB*, p. 49).[15] (The exaggeration is equally present in her own *Cuchulain of Muirthemne*, for which, as Declan Kiberd notes, Joyce felt 'a deep aversion').[16] History, in O'Grady's words, requires 'gigantic treatment' – the 'gigantic treatment of their history to which the bards were so addicted' (*H*, II.110). This is the Irish way of doing things, as, 'in the statue which fronts Trinity College, we have represented Grattan in twice or three times his natural size' (*HCP*, p. 236). In this kind of historiography, too, 'gigantism' goes hand in hand with a flight from and distaste for the actual. 'The distant in place and the distant in time', writes O'Grady, 'have ever been the chosen realms of the imagination' (*HCP*, p. 22). It was clearly those 'realms' that his own imagination preferred. Yet he also claims that there is more than imagination at stake. 'Historical or not,' he says of the Fenian heroes, 'they are real' (*HCP*, p. 355). This appears to leave him in the odd position of advocating an ideal history of ahistorical realities. Lady Gregory is similarly paradoxical and cavalier. 'The history of England and Ireland was shut out of the schools', she writes, in *The Kiltartan History Book*, 'and it became a passion'. She herself will merely record that impassioned history as it is already 'in "the Book of the People" '. But she will not 'go bail for the facts' (*KHB*, p. 51). Her logic dictates that history again float free of factuality. The political implications of this sort of attitude are evident enough. O'Grady, for instance, was always an ascendancy man, hostile to democratic ordinariness, to the demotic tendencies in Parnellite nationalism and the '*canaille*' or commercial classes.[17] Phillip Marcus points out that a chief attraction of

15 Foster remarks on a traditional Ascendancy 'culture of exaggeration' running back to the eighteenth century (Foster, p. 194).

16 Declan Kiberd, 'The Vulgarity of Heroics: Joyce's *Ulysses*', in *James Joyce: An International Perspective*, ed. Suheil Badi Bushrui and Bernard Benstock (Gerrards Cross, 1982), pp. 156–69.

17 E. A. Boyd, *Standish O'Grady: Selected Essays and Passages* (Dublin, n.d.), p. 46; quoted in Phillip L. Marcus, *Yeats and the Beginning of the Irish Renaissance* (London, 1970), p. 238. Cf. Lyons, pp. 33–5.

the old legends for enthusiasts was the refuge they offered from the sordor of the present.[18] But the legends also needed to be purged of more sordid, vulgar, and even obscene elements of their own. Ferguson and O'Grady were by no means alone in disliking these. 'We want the Irish spirit, certainly, in Irish literature,' wrote T. W. Rolleston, 'but we want its gold, not its dross.'[19] For O'Grady, the legends were and had to be an idealized haven to which 'the intellect of man, tired by contact with the vulgarity of actual things' could return 'for rest and recuperation' (*H*, I.22). On the other hand, to D. P. Moran, all the talk of 'ancient glories', of the Irish being 'a fine people long ago' that he saw as sanctioned 'by O'Curry and others' was mere arrant evasion of political realities.[20] Certainly, it is hard not to interpret it, at the very least, as partly an escapist reaction to the decline in ascendancy power.[21]

Crucially, Revival historiography sought to revitalize or rather to re-invent not only the ancient legends but ancient modes of history-telling: specifically, those of the bards. O'Grady did not merely use 'bardic story'. He also frequently attempted to employ 'the actual language of the bards, and as much as possible their style and general character of expression' (*H*, I.x). Indeed, he appears to have considered his own method bardic, his own work a continuation of bardic history, in which 'the legendary' continually blends 'with the historic narrative' (*H*, I.19). Lady Gregory was similarly fascinated by the bard as historian and, indeed, as teacher of history.[22] There was even a kind of identification with the bards as a privileged class 'entrusted with the preservation of the literature and history of the country' (*H*, II.50). Hyde shared this fascination, of course. Like Lady Gregory, Yeats, and Martyn, he was particularly interested in Raftery, seeing Raftery as a bardic historian able to keep the Irish appropriately conscious of Ireland. He praises Raftery's 'Story of the Bush' as 'a concise and intelligible history of Ireland' (and, it would seem, for Hyde, partly true history, too).[23] Of course, as a founder of the Gaelic League and its

18 Marcus, p. 224.

19 T. W. Rolleston, 'Shamrocks', *The Academy* (9 July 1887), p. 19; quoted in Marcus, p. 231.

20 D. P. Moran, *The Philosophy of Irish Ireland* (Dublin, 1905), p. 39.

21 Cf. Lyons, p. 72.

22 Lady Gregory, *Poets and Dreamers*, p. 10.

23 *Songs Ascribed to Raftery*, ed. and trans. Douglas Hyde (Dublin, 1903), p. 19. Cf. also Lady Gregory, 'Raftery' and 'West Irish Ballads', in *Poets and Dreamers*.

president until 1915, a believer in 'Gaelicism' and in the de-Anglicization of Irish literature, Hyde stands apart from the figures I have just been discussing. But he stands on their side, too: as Trinity-educated protestant, friend and collaborator of Yeats and Lady Gregory, firmly intent on keeping the League apolitical. Furthermore, his own grasp of Irish history as reflected in his *Literary History of Ireland*, though very different, say, to O'Grady's, is likewise reductive, and for similarly polemical purposes. It abstains altogether, for example, 'from any analysis or even mention of the works of Anglicized Irishmen of the last two centuries'.[24] Like O'Grady (and the bards, in O'Grady's view) Hyde is willing on the one hand to rely on ancient native sources (and to argue for that reliance) and, on the other, to 'leave verifiable history behind'.[25] At all events, some of Hyde's work clearly cannot simply be separated off from other aspects of Revival historiography. He shared and fed attitudes to history being developed by others, and this is particularly evident in his contribution to the cult of the bard.

One of the most striking contradictions in the kind of historical imagination I've been describing lies in its relation to English culture. In part, the intention was to draw further away from that culture and closer to an indigenous one.[26] O'Grady repeatedly states that this is one of his purposes. But in point of fact Englishness is constantly perceptible within the enterprise. That in itself reflects its compromises and its predicament. Marcus points out, for example, how earnestly Victorian Ferguson's whole conception of literature was.[27] England is constantly apparent in O'Grady's *History*, with its epigraphs from Shelley, Byron, and Keats, its outlandish stylistic oscillations between the plain historical, the pseudo-bardic, the high Shakespearian, and the would-be Miltonic. It is thus hardly surprising to find D. P. Moran asserting that the new historical enthusiasms have actually been accompanied by an increase in the Anglicization of Irish culture.[28] O'Grady's writing is very obviously Moran's 'mongrel thing'.[29] But contradiction was always bound to haunt this particular historical project. It sought to bridge gulfs, to heal divisions, to engineer the

24 Douglas Hyde, *A Literary History of Ireland from Earliest Times to the Present Day* (London, 1899), p. ix.

25 Hyde, *Literary History*, p. 239.

26 See Oliver McDonagh, *Ireland: The Union and Its Aftermath* (London, 1979), p. 72.

27 Marcus, p. 233.

28 Moran, p. 39.

29 Moran, p. 43.

fusion of cultures for which Yeats struggled. It attempted to minimize differences. Hence Lady Gregory's effort to imagine Irish tradition as a unity 'born of continuity of purpose' rather than a succession of disparate epochs ('The names change from age to age, that is all').[30] Actually, however, it was a historiography produced by a dominant but threatened class. Divided within itself, such writing, if anything, could only exacerbate the differences it sought to overcome.

Joyce was a middle-class Catholic intellectual, an ironic realist with a satirical intelligence and a devouring passion for exactitude. In his own distinctive way, he was politically radical and a nationalist, with a powerful feeling for the demotic. Revival historiography, its aesthetics and politics, were bound to seem anathema to him. As history, *Ulysses* itself is arguably a fierce struggle to reverse the emphases of Revivalist historiography and to reclaim Ireland and its past for Joyce's own culture. To O'Grady's idealist principles Joyce counterpoises a stubbornly realist aesthetic that insists on the significance of almost numberless historical particulars. To O'Grady's 'escape from positive history and unyielding despotic fact' (*HCP*, p. 57), he opposes a clear-eyed and resolute factuality. (Hence Stephen's battle: the 'nightmare' *is* 'despotic'). Where O'Grady dwells on ancient history and ignores the Catholic past, Joyce drastically economizes on allusions to ancient Ireland and fills his novel with accounts of and references to Irish Catholicism, its past, and its culture. To O'Grady's dismissal of the middle ages, Joyce opposes his own mediaevalism. O'Grady disparages what he takes to be the mediaeval 'thirst for minuteness, chronology and succession, co-ordination and relation' (*HCP*, p. 63). Joyce's Dantean aesthetic – his Dantean architectonics – promotes all these as values. Where O'Grady gives us the heroic, a history cleansed of meanness, squalor, and vulgarity, an art of gigantic inflation, Joyce offers the anti-heroic, the dirty, trivial, and obscene, an art of deflation. Where O'Grady's writing is contaminated by the very Englishness it seeks to resist, Joyce consciously and precisely relates parts of *Ulysses* to the supreme English literary genius (Shakespeare, in 'Scylla and Charybdis') and to the English literary tradition (in 'The Oxen of the Sun'). English culture gets contaminated itself in the process. Most strikingly of all, O'Grady sought to establish certain cultural connections between Ireland and ancient Greece, particularly Ireland and Homer. He repeatedly associates Irish bards with Homer, sees himself as writing Irish epic, and links that up with Homeric epic. Arguably, in

30 Lady Gregory, *Kiltartan Poetry Book*, p. iii.

incorporating a Homeric parallel into the structure of *Ulysses*, Joyce was partly countering O'Grady's Homeric analogies with a (wickedly ironic) one of his own.

Otherwise, Joyce's critique of the historical imagination of the Revival begins with Stephen in the 'Telemachiad'. As Stephen in his own person recasts and (half-mockingly) reinterprets the role of the bard, as he recasts Hyde (specifically, the translation of 'My Grief on the Sea'),[31] so too he also provides a kind of historical imagination in the 'Telemachiad' that is very different to that of the Revival. Stephen fleetingly gives form to episodes from a different Irish history to that of the Revival (or gives episodes of the same history a different form). But he is also infected by O'Grady. His tone and style, for instance, are sometimes remarkably close to O'Grady's (if noticeably superior versions). Even as late as 'The Oxen of the Sun', Stephen can sound very like O'Grady.[32] The point here is partly simple. Stephen is young. His 'blood', as 'Aeolus' tells us, is easily 'wooed by grace of language' (115/776). This in itself does something to explain the intermittent (and sometimes rich) ambiguities in Stephen's attitudes to the writing of Yeats, Hyde, O'Grady, even Russell. But the ambiguities leave the cultural and political critique looking somewhat less than wholly resolute. In the later episodes of *Ulysses*, it is necessarily conducted in a different manner – above all, in 'Cyclops'.

Insofar as it is possible to speak accurately of 'parody' in 'Cyclops', its most important targets are the styles of Revival historiography and related poetry and translation.[33] The very title of the episode, for example, and its 'technic' ('gigantism' – at least, according to the 1921 schema) refer us away to O'Grady. 'Cyclopean' and 'gigantic' were favourite adjectives of his. Joyce offers a mocking critique of Revival simulations of bardic history and discourse as found not only in Ferguson, O'Grady, Hyde, and Lady Gregory but in McCarthy, Samuel Lover, *et al.* Whole passages in 'Cyclops' allude to a composite mock-bardic set of styles and devices. Some have long been recognized as

31 *Ulysses* (Harmondsworth, 1986), p. 109/1.522–5: references are to this edition. Cf. *Love Songs of Connacht*, ed. and trans. Douglas Hyde (Dublin, 1893), pp. 29–31.

32 Cf. *Ulysses*, 322/376–80, for example, and O'Grady, *History of Ireland*, II.250–1.

33 'Parody' may not be the right word for much of what is going on in 'Cyclops' outside the naturalistic narrative. As in 'The Oxen of the Sun', Joyce actually mixes parody with pastiche, stylistic allusion, and specific forms of distortion of other styles.

such: the double epithets, for instance (as at 243/152–5), and the exaggerations of size; the lists or – to adopt the appropriate term as used by Hyde – 'runs'.[34] Joyce gives us a parodic 'fish-run' (241/71–3, 242/81–2), and the list of Nolan's wedding guests at 268/1268–78 is an outrageously eccentric parody of a 'tree-run'. He also compounds the hilarity – and the violation – by giving us a 'clergyman-run' (260–1/927–38) and *Catholic* runs, including a 'saint-run' (278/1671–1720). The list at 244/176–99, too, begins as a characteristic chronological run of names (and then develops quite aberrantly). Elsewhere we get the eulogistic catalogue of place-names, the *dindsenchas* that was common in bardic topography and Revival versions of it (242/110–12, 272/1452–61).[35] It is not surprising to find a comic passage that specifically treats of Hyde, Raftery, and the cult of the bard (256/712–39). Here, the humour of Garryowen's rann is directed less at Raftery than at Hyde's translatorese (which is certainly funny enough, at times). It is no accident, either, that Joyce humorously couples Raftery with Donal MacConsidine as a master of the 'satirical effusion' (256/728). MacConsidine was in fact no bard but the 'fine Irish scholar' referred to fleetingly in both *Love Songs of Connacht* and *Beside the Fire* as a transcriber of Gaelic poems.[36] Once again, the emphasis is on *versions of the original*, mediators and mediating forms.

Of course, there are moments when Joyce seems to be specifically parodying O'Grady's style (222/1183–90, for instance). He introduces words favoured by O'Grady, like 'puissant' (266/1184). He picks up on some of O'Grady's preferred designations – 'Banba' for Ireland, for example (248/375), and *Clanna Rury* for the Red Branch (as in 'O'Bloom, son of Rory', 245/216).[37] There are clear echoes in Joyce's introduction of the Citizen of O'Grady's manner of introducing his heroes (243/151–67).[38] Joyce also engineers subtle gratings of gear in his parodies, awkward little shifts in level that echo similar incongruities in O'Grady. One or two of the parodies even switch into a more anglicized mode, especially when a certain sort of English subject-matter is around, as if, again, a kind of comment is being passed

34 *Beside the Fire: A Collection of Irish Gaelic Folk Stories*, ed. and trans. Douglas Hyde (London, 1890), pp. xxv–vii.

35 Foster, p. 5.

36 See *Love Songs of Connacht*, pp. 11, 115, and *Beside the Fire*, p. xxxiii. The indications are that MacConsidine was little more than a scribe.

37 O'Grady prefers Banba to the comparable alternatives (Fohla and Eiré); Banba's particular associations were with physical beauty and fertility.

38 See, e.g., O'Grady, *History of Ireland*, II.215.

on O'Grady's kind of writing and its allegiances (246/290–300, 275–6/1593–1620). 'Cyclops', then, owes much to O'Grady's *History*, and to similar heroic Revival texts like *Gods and Fighting Men* and *Cuchulain of Muirthemne*. Thus the Citizen is very obviously placed as a Cuchulain-figure.[39] He has his Garryowen with him, as ancient heroes often have their hounds (Finn and his Bran, in particular).[40] A parodic voice gives him a spear and a 'strong growth' of hair, familiar attributes of ancient heroes (243/157, 244/200). It also dwells on 'the reverberations of his formidable heart', as O'Grady says of Cuchulain that 'like the sound of a mighty drum his heart beats' (243/165; *HCP*, p. 232). The throwing of the biscuit-tin is reminiscent of various flights of various missiles in the *History* and elsewhere. The ancient heroic duel finds its comic counterparts in 'Cyclops' in Bloom's dispute with the Citizen and the Bennett/Keogh fight (261/960–87). The account of the catastrophe in 'Cyclops' partly makes fun of similar accounts, like that of the catastrophe surrounding Cuchulain's death, in the *History* (281–2/1858–96; *H*, II.342). Bloom's departure down the Liffey and his surprise elevation to glory parody similar occasions in O'Grady and elsewhere. Finally, Bloom is set in a 'chariot', clearly Joyce's version of the ancient hero's war-car that, according to O'Grady, played such 'a vital and intimate' part in cyclic literature (282/1911; *HCP*, p. 31).

Joyce picks up other topoi, too: Ireland's fruitfulness (242/102–117), its rich afforestation (268/1266–79), sport, brewing (246/280–6), and the ancient law (265/1111–40). The fact that they are topoi is important. In 'Cyclops', it is not specific allusions that really count, nor a particular butt, not even O'Grady. Rather, the episode is a gigantic recycling of a stock in trade. Joyce was making light of a whole mode of discourse that speciously presented itself as a form of historiography. The 'making light' was a conscious tactic. Revival history had effectively colonized a set of narratives. It had appropriated an indigenous, bardic tradition for its own ends. Whilst claiming that it was bodying forth the soul of Ireland, it continued to rely heavily on Anglo-Irish and – secondarily – English cultural constructs. Linguistically, much of the humour in 'Cyclops' is at the expense of clumsy attempts to match Gaelic idiom with a sort of 'approximate English'. It was precisely that 'approximation' where there was and could be no real proximity that Joyce would have no truck with. His

39 Noted by, e.g., Schwarz, p. 178.

40 Cf. Herring, pp. 134–5, for an appropriate passage from O'Grady.

laughter refuses to accept the validity of the Revival enterprise. Rather, it pushes it back, relativizes it, mockingly demonstrates its cultural shallowness. It also offers a critique. Into the formulae to which Revival historiography resorted Joyce introduces precisely what it sought to exclude: Catholicism, the middle ages, the colonial past and present, too. He also strews his episode with all kinds of references to matters English. It is as if he wished to emphasize the actual, compromised, adulterated nature of a history and culture that the Revival had attempted to purify, but only at the cost of evasion and massive omission. As for Joyce heroic and gigantic forms required deflation, so too the forms of an idealist history had to be defaced with the marks of what they had sought to hold at bay.

There is another important way, too, in which the process at work in 'Cyclops' is a fiercely and deliberately corrupting one. O'Grady was by no means altogether enthusiastic about the original narratives from which he derived so much. He found them often 'wild and improbable', for instance, 'weird with incursions', full of 'the shifting chaos of obscure epic tale'. He himself wished, on the other hand, 'to mould all into a harmonious and reasonable form' (*HCP*, pp. 202–3). At the very outset of the *History* he explicitly refuses simply to 'pile up' a mass of bardic material. For such a mass would be 'without harmony, meaning or order. The valuable and the valueless', he writes, would be promiscuously mingled together, and the whole 'would be utterly incondite, inorganic', strewn with incongruities and probably 'unreadable' (*H*, I.ix). Rather, the old bardic narratives must be purged, purified, condensed, shaped. Phillip Marcus has shown in detail how far this process often went in Revival versions of the ancient tales. They were moralized, cleansed of various elements originally intrinsic to them: the obscene, the comic, the fantastic, grotesque, monstrous, and frivolous.[41] The original Cuchulain, for example, was an extraordinary figure. According to Rhys, his contortions – in the course of his battle-frenzy, at least – were so many and various that they 'won for him the nickname of the *Riastartha*, or the Distorted One'.[42] But none

41 Marcus, pp. 228–37.

42 John Rhys, *Lectures on the Origin and Growth of Religion as Illustrated by Celtic Heathendom* (London, 1888), p. 438. Rhys says of the original Cuchulain that 'when he got thoroughly angry with his antagonists, the calves of his legs would twist round till they were where his shins should have been; his mouth became large enough to contain a man's head; his liver and his lungs could be seen swinging in his throat and mouth; every hair on his body became as sharp as a thorn, and a drop of blood or a spark of fire stood on each; one of his eyes

of this appears in the *History*. O'Grady, De Vere, P. W. Joyce all modified plots, too, tidied characterization up, did their best to provide a 'good story'.[43] In doing so, they produced a much more homogenous and orthodox form of narrative than that of the legendary tales themselves.

Again, Joyce works in the opposite direction. He introduces into his 'Cyclops' narrative the very qualities in bardic literature that the Revival writers had so often sought to excise from their texts: vulgarity, for instance, grotesqueness, prodigious bizarrerie of a kind that we would look for in vain in O'Grady, let alone in Ferguson. If the presence of Rabelais in *Ulysses* is felt most in 'Cyclops', there is an obvious reason for it.[44] Joyce is using a Rabelaisian 'gigantism' – a mediaeval and Catholic one – to criticize but also modify and indeed transform its Revival equivalent. Joyce does it, however, in a way that pushes the latter back closer to the spirit – at least at certain points – of the original. So, too, Joyce restores *heterogeneity* as a narrative principle: the 'alternating asymmetry', for instance, that was one of the 'technics' he ascribed to the episode;[45] the abrupt slides into nonsense, irrelevance, or triviality, as in the case of the Black Liz passage (259/846–9); the casual confusions (in some of the lists) of the grandiose and the insignificant (as at 244/176–99), like those in similar lists in 'Story of the Bush';[46] the multiplicity of the parodies and parodic styles; the variability itself in the relation between the parodies and the styles they allude to. All make 'Cyclops' look the very antithesis of – say – *Gods and Fighting Men*, with its smooth, flat prose and its uniform point of view. O'Grady aspired to an ideal harmony. Joyce insisted on dissonance and discord. Historically, of course, he was right. But the insistence also makes his cultural allegiances clearer. For in his resistance to Anglo-Irish appropriation, Joyce also revitalizes or finds a modern equivalent for certain properties of bardic narrative

became as small as a needle's, or else it sank back into his head further than a heron could have reached with its beak, while the other protruded itself to a corresponding length'.

43 Marcus, pp. 228–37 *passim*.

44 Lawrence sees Joyce as 'more Rabelaisian in 'Cyclops' than in any other chapter of *Ulysses*' (Lawrence, p. 109).

45 According to the Linati schema. See Ellmann's comparison of the Linati and Gorman-Gilbert schemas in his *Ulysses on the Liffey* (London, 1972), pp. 187–9.

46 See *Songs Ascribed to Raftery*, p. 121.

itself. In other words, he positively wrests a tradition back from the hands that have sought to seize it.

But Joyce is also prepared to use other weapons against Revival historiography. Historical particularity is one of the most obvious. Where O'Grady rejects 'minuteness' on the one hand and 'despotic fact' on the other, the historical allusions in some of the parodies in 'Cyclops' are extremely precise.[47] Thus the passage that parodies the Creed, for example, is exact in its reference to the contemporary controversy over naval discipline (270/1354–9).[48] Such historical precision also partly serves as something of an antidote to the Citizen's often generalized, emotional, error-strewn rhodomontade. The 'Alaki of Abeakuta' passage, with its clever pastiche of Griffith that actually identifies with Griffith as satirist, has a similar effect to the 'Creed' passage (274/1514–33). Joyce appears to share something of the Citizen's anti-Englishness here. But his own has a hard exactitude that the Citizen's diatribes lack. The instrument used to counter the Citizen's use of history here is thus the same as that employed against Revival historiography. This offers a fresh perspective on Joyce's treatment of the Citizen. Critical views of the latter have usually been negative. On occasions, English and sometimes American commentators have seemed merely to be resorting to familiar stereotypes. Of course, there have been more high-minded versions of this: the kind of reading, for instance, that suggests that, through Bloom on the one hand and irony on the other, Joyce subjects the Citizen and nationalism to a severe but warranted humanist critique.[49] But this kind of interpretation surely relies on a tired old Leavisite hermeneutic that bears little or no relevance to Joyce's endeavour. It is possible to point out, by way of rejoinder, that there is an element of crude satire and indeed of crude *insult* in the writing of 'Cyclops' itself that markedly closes the gap between Joyce and the Citizen (see, for instance, 282/1894). One might also note, with Ellmann, that the Triestine

47 For an account of allusions of this kind, see F. L. Radford, 'King, Pope and Hero-Martyr: *Ulysses* and the Nightmare of Irish History', *James Joyce Quarterly*, 15 (1978), pp. 275–323.

48 See R. M. Adams, *Surface and Symbol: The Consistency of James Joyce's Ulysses* (New York, 1962), p. 227; and Don Gifford and Robert J. Seidman, *Ulysses Annotated: Notes for James Joyce's Ulysses* (London, 1988), p. 357.

49 See, e.g., Parrinder, p. 172; S. L. Goldberg, *The Classical Temper: A Study of James Joyce's Ulysses* (London, 1961), pp. 282–3; Matthew Hodgart, *James Joyce: A Student's Guide* (London, 1978), pp. 101–2; Schwarz, pp. 175–6, 180–1; and Ellmann, *Ulysses on the Liffey*, p. 116.

lectures (and, indeed, the Defoe lecture) show how close to the Citizen Joyce could sometimes sound.[50] But, helpful though this may be, it is nonetheless to continue to think in terms of Joyce's 'judgment of' and/or 'sympathy' or 'lack of sympathy' with his creation. It is surely more important to recognize that Joyce *understands* the Citizen (historically), and invites a particular understanding of him by placing him in a certain context. In particular, he recognizes the extent to which the Citizen's view of history – which so preoccupies him in 'Cyclops' – carries on from and is conditioned by the view of history so frequently adumbrated in the 'parodies'. The areas of historical concern may be different. Nonetheless, as some good Joyce commentary has recently indicated, it is important to remember how deeply implicated the older Revivalism was in the new nationalism, and how relevant to Joyce this is.[51] 'Cyclops' makes that implication clear. To some extent, it does so in simple ways. Thus traces of the 'composite style' evident in the parodies also appear in what the Citizen has to say. The double epithets are there, for example (266–7/1198–1200). So, at odd moments, is the choice and archaic vocabulary (270/1375). The place-list is there (269/1302) and so is the 'run' (267–8/1240–54). Beyond that, the habits of imprecision (267/1240) and exaggeration (267/1199–1205) sometimes look the same. Likewise, the specific historical lacunae may be different, but the tendency to leave lacunae is familiar (270/1365–75). So is the construction of crude oppositions (251/523–4) and the reliance on a mythology (269/1306–10). Some of the themes in the parodies and their sources are equally themes of the Citizen's: sport (260/889–90), Irish afforestation (268/1262–4), the fruitfulness of Ireland (267–8/1242–54). More importantly, the heroic vision of Revival historiography spills over into the Citizen's nationalist account of history. The fondness for heroics is still there (270/1372–5), along with the same grandiose nostalgia (268/1248–54) and the same grandiosely improbable view of the future (260/891). Joyce was well aware of the connections binding the emergent nationalist culture to Revival culture.[52] He was also well aware of the latent

50 Ellmann, *James Joyce* (Oxford, 1982), p. 258.

51 See, e.g., Kiberd, *passim*; Seamus Deane, ' "Masked with Matthew Arnold's Face": Joyce and Liberalism', in *James Joyce: The Centennial Symposium*, ed. Morris Beja, Phillip Herring, Maurice Harmon, and David Norris (Chicago, 1986), pp. 9–21 *passim*; and G. J. Watson, 'The Politics of *Ulysses*', in *Joyce's Ulysses: The Larger Perspective*, ed. Robert D. Newman and Weldon Thornton (London, 1987), pp. 39–59 *passim*.

52 Cf. Lyons, pp. 85–8.

continuities between their respective views of history. The relationship between the two cultures partly resembled that between Revival culture and English culture. The demands were repeatedly for purity. The reality, again and again – as Joyce himself was underlining – was complicity.

Almost everything else in 'Cyclops' can be fitted around its central concerns as I have described them: the parody of Russell and theosophical discourse, for instance (another Revivalist rejection of 'the vulgarity of actual things' and of history along with it, 267–8/1240–54); the humour at the expense of Griffith's *The Resurrection of Hungary* and the 'Hungarian parallel' in general (for Joyce, another absurdly grandiose form of historical discourse, 276/1635–7, 280–1/1814–42).[53] Joyce's seriocomic treatment of Bloom in 'Cyclops' also makes more sense in this context.[54] It remains perplexing only if we insist on seeing Bloom and the realist narrative as central to the meaning of the episode. Take the historical theme and the parodies as a starting point, and it becomes clear that Joyce's presentation of Bloom is ambiguous and playful simply because he can afford it to be. There is only a limited amount at stake. In a way, he takes what Bloom says seriously – he means it – but it is clearly not intended to carry an overly large burden of significance in the episode. Finally, once we take the ramifications of the historical theme fully into account, the distinctive contribution of the nameless narrator to the meaning of 'Cyclops' becomes clearer. In tone and manner he is the antithesis of the value-system and the imaginative world of O'Grady, Yeats, and Lady Gregory (and particularly of their anti-democratic tendencies). He is equally obviously a reaction against the Citizen's or – say – Griffith's or Pearse's view of the Irish.[55] Critical responses to him have surely been too prim and proper.[56] We should find him a liberatingly comic relief, not only after the Citizen, but after the parodies and the literature to which they are a reaction. His limitations are doubtless

53 On the Hungarian-Irish 'Parallel', see Thomas Kabdebo, *The Hungarian-Irish 'Parallel' and Arthur Griffith's Use of his Sources* (Maynooth, 1988).

54 Noted by, e.g., James H. Maddox, *Joyce's Ulysses and the Assault upon Character* (Hassocks, 1978), pp. 87–8; Goldberg, p. 132; and Kenner, pp. 255–6; the view is widespread.

55 As evident in Griffith's response to Synge, *In the Shadow of the Glen* and *The Playboy of the Western World*.

56 See, e.g., Ellmann, *The Consciousness of Joyce* (London, 1977), p. 21; *Ulysses on the Liffey*, pp. 110–11; Peake, p. 234; and Stanley Sultan, *The Argument of Ulysses* (New York, 1964), pp. 234–6.

chronic. But for Joyce, in contrast to a whole historiography – a whole mode of the historical imagination – he has and represents a vulgar and vital presentness. He himself has no sense of history at all. But he and his discourse embody Joyce's wicked challenge to the historical imagination of others. For here, Joyce is saying, is an actual Irishman, living in history, and you must take him warts and all.

Virginia Woolf, History, and the Metaphors of Orlando

AVRIL HORNER

Virginia Woolf's *Orlando* takes great liberties with history. Closely modelled on the life of Vita Sackville-West, it is often at odds with the main source of its material – not least in allowing Orlando to live for over three hundred years and change sex at the age of thirty. Yet *Orlando* records and preserves Vita's character and inclinations with affectionate accuracy. Among other things, Vita Sackville-West loved literature, elk-hounds, driving cars, Knole, gardening, and a rope of pearls which she wore round her neck constantly. She was physically clumsy, somewhat aloof in her aristocratic bearing, and occasionally emphasized her rather androgynous appearance by wearing corduroy breeches. In 1927, at the age of thirty-five, she was awarded the Hawthornden prize for literature for her poem, 'The Land'. Throughout her life she conducted passionate affairs with women, including an intense relationship with Virginia Woolf during the years 1922–1929.[1] Her marriage to the writer and diplomat, Harold Nicolson, by whom she had two sons, was both happy and unconventional. These aspects of her life and personality, metamorphosed slightly, are accurately recorded in *Orlando*, as are certain features of her much loved family home.[2] Yet the main grief of Vita Sackville-

1 See Victoria Glendinning, *Vita: The Life of V. Sackville-West* (London, 1983); Nigel Nicolson, *Portrait of a Marriage* (London, 1973); Joanne Trautmann, *The Jessamy Brides: The Friendship of Virginia Woolf and V. Sackville-West* (Pennsylvania, 1973); and Jean O. Love, '*Orlando* and Its Genesis: Venturing and Experimenting in Art, Love, and Sex', in *Virginia Woolf: Revaluation and Continuity*, ed. Ralph Freedman (Berkeley and London, 1980), pp. 189–218.

2 In a letter dated 3 January 1923, Woolf thanks Vita Sackville-West for sending her a copy of *Knole and the Sackvilles* which Vita had published in 1922 (*Letters of Virginia Woolf, Volume III: 1923–1928*, ed. Nigel Nicolson and Joanne Trautmann (London, 1977), p. 1); Woolf's description of Orlando's ancestral home clearly owes much to her reading of Vita's book. See also Frank Baldanza, '*Orlando* and the Sackvilles', *PMLA*, 70 (1955), pp. 274–9; and David Bonnell Green, '*Orlando* and the Sackvilles: Addendum', *PMLA*, 71 (1956), pp. 268–9.

West's life – the fact that she was unable to inherit the Sackville family home of Knole in Kent simply because she was a woman – is excised from Orlando's story. Instead, Orlando, to her great joy, is allowed to retain the huge country mansion which, true to its original, is given to a Sackville ancestor by Queen Elizabeth I. *Orlando* does not, then, conform to the ideal of biography as an accurate record of one person's life. It is similarly impossible to read the book as any exact history of England: though the broad brush strokes catch 'the spirit' of the years 1588 to 1928, there are disconcerting 'mistakes' of detail which lend the work an air of *capriccio*. Several critics have commented on the historical anachronisms of *Orlando*: Raymond Mortimer, reviewing *Orlando* in 1929, noted that 'old St. Paul's is given a dome and dahlias flower in England in the seventeenth century'; Beverley Schlack has pointed out that Orlando is reading the works of Sir Thomas Browne at a time when the 'Doctor of Norwich' would have been no more than a child; Alice Fox has complained that Woolf's Jacobeans should not be dancing a quadrille.[3] In June 1930, Woolf wrote a short letter to Ernest Rhys, the poet and editor of Everyman's Library, thanking him for his kind remarks on *Orlando* and commenting rather ruefully, 'If you knew how many letters I get pointing out the mistakes in that book, you would understand that your appreciation is very valuable'.[4]

In the face of such a cavalier attitude to biography and chronology, what is the reader to make of Woolf's attitude to history? Vita Sackville-West found *Orlando* 'unique', commenting that 'it dazzles and bewilders me'.[5] Many readers since then have shared Virginia Woolf's own perception of it as 'a joke . . . a writers [*sic*] holiday';[6] others have seen it as 'simply a piece of mystification'[7] or an irritatingly self-

3 See respectively Raymond Mortimer, 'Virginia Woolf and Lytton Strachey' (*Bookman*, New York), in *Virginia Woolf: The Critical Heritage*, ed. Robin Majumdar and Allen McLaurin (London, 1975), p. 242; Beverly Ann Schlack, *Continuing Presences: Virginia Woolf's Use of Literary Allusion* (Pennslyvania and London, 1979), p. 172; Alice Fox, *Virginia Woolf and the Literature of the English Renaissance* (Oxford, 1990), p. 161.

4 *Letters IV: 1929–1931* (London, 1978), p. 178.

5 Glendinning, p. 202.

6 Entry for 18 March 1928, *The Diary of Virginia Woolf, Volume 3: 1925–30*, ed. Anne Olivier Bell (London, 1980; Harmondsworth, 1987), p. 177.

7 Paul Dottin, 'Les Sortilèges de Virginia Woolf' (*Revue de France*, Paris), in *Woolf: The Critical Heritage*, p. 254.

indulgent fantasy. All these reactions preclude any consideration of *Orlando* as having anything serious or interesting to say about history and historiography, a fact which Virginia Woolf anticipated in her diary comment on the work: 'It may fall between two stools, be too long for a joke, & too frivolous for a serious book' (*Diary*, III. 177). She clearly felt, however, that it did have a serious side: in the middle of writing *Orlando* she reflected on its progress and re-affirmed her intention that 'its spirit' was to be 'satiric' (*Diary*, III. 168). Recent feminist critics, alert to *Orlando* as an exploration of androgyny and the social construction of sexuality, have become very interested in this 'serious' side of the book. They have suggested that Woolf's work challenges fixed assumptions concerning gender and even that it anticipates the work of feminist theorists such as Julia Kristeva.[8]

More recent readers have also recognized that Orlando's refusal to die allows Woolf to consider the effect of historical determinism on the writer (for whatever else changes, Orlando always wishes to write) and – since Orlando is female for at least two of the three hundred years or so covered by the novel – in particular, upon the *woman* writer. Gillian Beer points out in her essay, 'Beyond Determinism: George Eliot and Virginia Woolf', that 'Death may become the only means of escape from the determining bonds of a particular society – especially is this so if the author subscribes intellectually to the idea of determinism'.[9] In Woolf's first novel, *The Voyage Out* (1915), Rachel Vinrace's death suggests precisely such an escape: English society at the turn of the century wishes her to conform to the pattern of marriage and motherhood; it has no place for her bisexuality and serious commitment to music. In *Orlando*, the hero/ine escapes such a fate by

8 For recent feminist work on *Orlando* that deals with the social construction of gender, see Sandra M. Gilbert, 'Costumes of the Mind: Transvestism as Metaphor in Modern Literature', in *Writing and Sexual Difference*, ed. Elizabeth Abel (Brighton, 1982), pp. 193–219; Mary Jacobus, *Reading Women: Essays in Feminist Criticism* (London, 1986; 1987), pp. 3–24; Judy Little, '(En)gendering laughter: Woolf's *Orlando* as contraband in the age of Joyce', in *Last Laughs: Perspectives on Women and Comedy*, ed. Regina Barreca (New York and London, 1988), pp. 179–91. For work which argues that Woolf's writing anticipates Kristevan theory, see Toril Moi, *Sexual/Textual Politics* (London and New York, 1985), pp. 1–18; and Makiko Minow-Pinkney, *Virginia Woolf & The Problem of the Subject: Feminine Writing in the Major Novels* (Brighton, 1987), espec. pp. 129–51.

9 Gillian Beer, *Arguing with the Past: Essays in Narrative from Woolf to Sidney* (London and New York, 1989), p. 125.

transcending death; the comic mode allows Woolf a different solution to the same problems of social determinism.

However, Orlando's panoramic view across history enables Woolf not only to consider the creation of the subject within specific historical moments, but also to exercise her own attitudes to historical periods, historiography, and the relationship between literature and history. We know, for example, that Woolf had read several historical studies of Queen Elizabeth and had reviewed at least one.[10] We also know, from a letter written in February 1926 (*Letters*, III. 242), that she had discussed with Lytton Strachey his portrait of the Queen in his forthcoming book, *Elizabeth and Essex: A Tragic History*. When the work appeared in December 1928 – two months or so after the publication of *Orlando* – she pronounced it a 'lively superficial meretricious book' and six months later congratulated herself in her diary: 'dashing off *Orlando* I had done better than he had done' (*Diary*, III. 208, 234). The forceful and charismatic Elizabeth who appears in *Orlando*, and whose ghost is welcomed into Knole on the last page (during what was historically the reign of George V), is indeed a far cry from the sexually neurotic and indecisive monarch of Strachey's work. Woolf's portrait gives us not only a lively literary cameo, but also an alternative 'history' of Queen Elizabeth I.

Orlando can, indeed, be seen as a feminist revision of English literature and history so long as we understand that for Woolf this meant restoring a lost balance between the sexes rather than trumpeting the superiority of her own; the narrator of *Orlando* comments sharply, we might remember here, on the 'extreme folly – than which none is more distressing in woman or man either – of being proud of her sex' (p. 100).[11] In a story written in 1906 Woolf created a woman historian, Rosamund Merridew, a specialist in the legal minutiae of 'the system of land tenure in medieval England', who is distracted from her research by a fifteenth-century manuscript entitled 'The Journal of Mistress Joan Martyn'. This journal records how Joan Martyn and her mother manage the land and the people while the men are away at war; they see themselves as rulers 'of a small island set in the midst of turbulent waters'. Joan's record of the seasons, the weather, and the relationships of the small community is shot through with references

10 See Fox, *Woolf and the Literature of the English Renaissance*, pp. 166–7.

11 All quotations are from *Orlando: A Biography* (London: Grafton, 1977; 1985).

to ballads, stories, and songs which she sees as 'authentic' records of human experience. Joan loses faith, however, in the importance of her own journal – 'truly, there is nothing in the pale of my days that needs telling' – and vows that if she ever writes again, it will be of 'Knights and Ladies and of adventures in strange lands'.[12] Joan Martyn's journal offers an alternative notion of 'history' to that embraced by Rosamund Merridew and by John Martyn, the owner of the manuscript and a man who is fascinated by past wars and financial transactions. This story marks Woolf's early awareness of how literary texts compete with historical texts as narratives of the past; it also intimates how a woman's text can intervene between the two so as to challenge the privileged status of received history – a history which often confines itself to accounts of governments, reigns, and wars. Joan Martyn's 'tenure' of both her home and her place in history is altogether more fragile than the legal tenure studied by Rosamund Merridew, but her journal communicates the spirit of life in the fifteenth century with more energy and vividness than any legal document.

Even Woolf's early fiction, then, suggests that she perhaps shared Catherine Morland's view of received history as

> '. . . very tiresome; and yet I often think it odd that it should be so dull, for a great deal of it must be invention. The speeches that are put into the heroes' mouths, their thoughts and designs – the chief of all this must be invention, and invention is what delights me in other books.'[13]

In *Orlando*, invention and fantasy play a large part in Woolf's revision of England's literary history, which at the same time reminds us that the received version is itself partly invention. Mockingly adopting the tone of a scholarly historian at the opening of Chapter III, the narrator admits that in order to reconstruct, from the surviving damaged 'manuscripts' and 'fragments', Orlando's life in Constantinople during the reign of Charles II, she is forced 'to speculate, to surmise, and even to use the imagination' (p. 75). Writing to Clive Bell in January 1928, Woolf commented: 'Does it not strike you that history is one of the most fantastic concoctions of the human brain? That it bears the

12 Virginia Woolf, 'The Journal of Mistress Joan Martyn', in *Virginia Woolf: The Complete Shorter Fiction*, ed. Susan Dick (London, 1987), pp. 48, 86, 89. I am grateful to Sue Zlosnik for pointing out the relevance of this story to a discussion of Woolf's attitudes to history and historiography.

13 Jane Austen, *Northanger Abbey* (Harmondsworth, 1972; 1974), p. 123.

remotest likeness to the truth seems to me unthinkable' (*Letters*, III. 454). Historical 'truth', in fact, is best left to the poets and the novelists:

> To give a truthful account of London society at that or indeed at any other time, is beyond the powers of the biographer or the historian. Only those who have little need of the truth, and no respect for it – the poets and the novelists – can be trusted to do it, for this is one of the cases where the truth does not exist. Nothing exists. The whole thing is a miasma – a mirage. (p. 120)

Woolf furthers this mood of scepticism by giving us a self-conscious narrator who, as we shall see, refuses to take seriously the supposed objectivity of the historian or biographer and clearly places herself historically as a woman writing in England during the years 1927 and 1928.

I want now to turn from these wider issues to the text itself and to suggest that Woolf's sceptical attitude to history is obliquely but effectively expressed in the metaphorical structure of *Orlando*. Among the most interesting metaphors of the work are those of ice, water, the country house, and birds; also important are voyages and the sense of vista which frequently informs the work. This last element adds a geographically comic dimension to the fantastic nature of *Orlando*. Occasionally vistas are realistically presented: Orlando's view of London on her return to England during the reign of Queen Anne, for example, with 'Greenwich Hospital erected in memory of Queen Mary by her husband, his late majesty, William the Third', is quite convincing and corrects an earlier architectural anachronism since, we are told, Orlando can now see 'the dome of St. Paul's which Mr. Wren had built in her absence' (p. 103). More frequently, however, panoramic views, which seem comfortably possible at first, dissolve into quite impossible perspectives. We learn that Orlando frequently seeks out hill tops and high places and that s/he 'loved solitary places, vast views' (p. 12); we are also informed, several times, that her eyesight is 'hawklike' in its sharpness. However, we can only gasp on learning that from the viewpoint of the oak tree at Knole, Orlando can see 'nineteen English counties . . . and on clear days thirty or perhaps forty' (p. 12); that from a mountain top in Turkey she can see 'far off, across the Sea of Marmara, the plains of Greece, and . . . the Acropolis with a white streak or two, which must, she thought, be the Parthenon' (p. 90); that a final sighting from the oak tree at Knole allows her to take in 'Snowdon's crags . . . the far Scottish hills and the wild tides that swirl about the Hebrides' (p. 203). Gleefully disrupting any suspension of disbelief, Woolf reminds her reader, through metaphor, that *Orlando* is not just fantasy: it is also about 'our view of the world and the world's view of us' (p. 117).

That 'view of the world' is influenced by factors such as gender, nationality, class, and historical moment. Woolf recognized that biography and history are both prey to an inevitable subjectivity and thus cannot deal with 'truth' in any absolute sense. She also recognized the roots of her own prejudices, seeing in herself an affinity with the writing of the Elizabethan age and an impatience with the Victorians. Associating her own immediate past, the late Victorian age, with stifling convention and sexual hypocrisy, she found the energy, economy, and frankness of Elizabethan literature exciting and liberating. In December 1929, she wrote in her Diary:

> Now, with this load despatched, I am free to begin reading Elizabethans . . . This thought fills me with joy – no overstatement . . . It was the Elizabethan prose writers I loved first & most wildly, stirred by Hakluyt, which father lugged home for me . . . (III. 270–1)

This very subjective attitude to the past and its literature is clearly present in *Orlando* and life in England is exaggerated accordingly. During Orlando's time as a young man in Elizabethan and Jacobean England, the skies are blue, the landscapes brilliant, life full of passion and energy. The skies of Victorian England, however, are cloudy and its houses damp. As Woolf confessed in a letter to Vita Sackville-West in 1929, 'the climate changes in sympathy with the age' (*Letters*, IV. 100).

Thus Virginia Woolf's own predilections clearly inform the history of England as it is presented in *Orlando*, a work in which prejudices and anachronisms are writ large in order to call into question the supposed objectivity of the historian. Indeed, with some amusement, Virginia Woolf deliberately draws attention to her own historical position and speculates on what it will not allow her to say: 'But let other pens treat of sex and sexuality; we quit such odious subjects as soon as we can' (p. 87). A hundred years or so after Jane Austen, she finds that there are still certain areas which are textually out of bounds to her as a writing woman. Discussing the topic more seriously in the essay 'Professions for Women' (1931), she comments that

> telling the truth about my own experience as a body, I do not think I solved. I doubt that any woman has solved it yet. The obstacles

> against her are still immensely powerful – and yet they are very difficult to define.[14]

At one point in this essay, these 'obstacles' are represented by the phantom of the Angel in the House who, with her insistence that she be charming and conciliatory to her male colleagues, inhibits the woman writer's critical faculty and artistic honesty. In *Orlando*, the same 'obstacles' are represented by the figures of Purity, Chastity, and Modesty who appear when Orlando changes sex and who are ironically invoked by the narrator when the hero/ine becomes a mother. In the first instance they try to draw a veil over the proceedings in an attempt to defy those 'austere Gods' of Truth, Candour, and Honesty (p. 84); clearly they are associated with late Victorian ideas of the 'feminine' and the evolution of sexual hypocrisy. Their failure to appear in 1928 when Orlando gives birth leads the narrator to create, in a spirit of self-irony, another 'veil' which will enforce society's silent censorship of Orlando's 'experiences as a body':

> Is nothing then, going to happen this pale March morning to mitigate, to veil, to cover, to conceal, to shroud this undeniable event whatever it may be? For after giving that sudden, violent start, Orlando – but Heaven be praised, at this very moment there struck up outside one of these frail, reedy, fluty, jerky, old-fashioned barrel-organs which are still sometimes played by Italian organ-grinders in back streets. (p. 183)

There follows an extraordinary quasi-Joycean epiphany concerning a barrel-organ and a kingfisher. Parody, digression, and 'veil', this passage nevertheless contains hidden within it the language of sexuality and childbirth:

> gasps and groans . . . bulbs, hairy and red, thrust into the earth in October; flowering now . . . the splendid fulfilment of natural desires . . . tear us asunder and wound us and split us apart . . . he flys [*sic*], burns, bursts the seal of sleep . . . so that now floods back refluent like a tide , the red, thick stream of life again . . . 'It's a very fine boy, M'lady,' said Mrs. Banting, the midwife, putting her first-born child into Orlando's arms. (pp. 183–5)

14 *Virginia Woolf: Women & Writing*, introduced Michèle Barrett (London, 1979), p. 62.

Woolf here both acknowledges and satirizes those 'mystic boundaries', as she described them in *Three Guineas*,[15] which prevent her narrator from documenting certain areas of experience. She thus places herself historically and draws attention to her own limitations as historian and biographer. These restrictions are also reflected by Orlando's experience as a woman writing in the twentieth century. Working on a passage in 'The Oak' (actually four lines taken *verbatim* from Vita Sackville-West's 'The Land'),[16] Orlando sensuously describes some fritillaries as 'Egyptian girls' – but then feels

> some power (remember we are dealing with the most obscure manifestations of the human spirit) reading over her shoulder, and when she had written 'Egyptian girls', the power told her to stop. Grass, the power seemed to say, going back with a ruler such as governesses use to the beginning, is all right; the hanging cups of fritillaries – admirable; the snaky flower – a thought, strong from a lady's pen, perhaps, but Wordsworth, no doubt, sanctions it; but – girls? Are girls necessary? You have a husband at the Cape, you say? Ah, well, that'll do. (p. 166)

Woolf's usual optimism concerning the freedom offered to women by the twentieth century is tempered, then, by her awareness that the restraints internalized by women still fetter them intellectually and artistically. Literature and history written in such circumstances must, inevitably, be shaped by their moment of production.

Woolf's use of parody and pastiche in *Orlando* provides further confirmation of her 'view of the world'. These elements suggest unashamedly partisan reactions to previous literary representations of experience and to 'the spirit of the age' that produced them. Thus Thomas Dekker's description of the winter of 1608, 'virtually unknown before its publication in one of Woolf's favourite anthologies, Edward Arber's *An English Garner*', according to Alice Fox,[17] feeds into Woolf's description of the Great Frost which takes on a fantastic and incredible dimension in *Orlando*. Dekker's mention of 'costermongers

15 Virginia Woolf, *Three Guineas* (London, 1986), p. 121.

16 For the four lines of poetry on p. 166 of *Orlando*, see V. Sackville-West, *Collected Poems* (New York, 1934), p. 58: the erotic quality of this passage is more evident in the lines that follow in which the 'Egyptian girl' is described as 'Holding her captive close with her bare brown arms,/Close to her little breast beneath the silk' (p. 59).

17 Fox, *Woolf and the Literature of the English Renaissance*, p. 159.

to serve you at your call' on the frozen Thames and his reports of people who sank into the river and 'never rose to the top again',[18] become transmuted in *Orlando* into the 'old bumboat woman' who, drowned in an accident the previous autumn, can now be seen through the frozen depths 'for all the world as if she were about to serve a customer, though a certain blueness about the lips hinted the truth' (p. 23). However, although the England of Elizabeth and James is a place of death, it is also one of vigorous life, as Orlando's tempestuous relationship with the exotic Sasha demonstrates; Woolf's portrayal of England at this time suggests an admiration for the age's frankness about matters of death and sexuality as she perceives it through the literature of the time. It is no coincidence that the play which Orlando and Sasha go to watch during the winter of 1608 is *Othello* – the same play which allows Clarissa Dalloway obliquely to express her suppressed love for Sally Seton. The Elizabethan dramatists, according to Woolf, 'had an attitude to life which made them able to express themselves freely and fully . . . they never make us feel . . . that there is anything hindering, hampering, inhibiting the full current of their minds'.[19]

Use of pastiche and parody elsewhere is similarly judgemental. We learn in chapter V that 'the spirit of the nineteenth century was antipathetic to [Orlando] in the extreme' (p. 152); Woolf enacts her own revenge and that of Orlando, however, not by simply rejecting the Victorians but, as Gillian Beer has pointed out, by rewriting them. Thus, as Beer has noted,[20] a passage from Ruskin's *Modern Painters* (1843) is comically appropriated and its tragic intimations undercut: the massive and sublime nature of Ruskin's cloudy sky is, in Woolf's work, more prosaically associated with a dampness of the heart and mind which leads to a peculiar mental inertia and an overblown literary style. Later in the same chapter, both *Wuthering Heights* and *Jane Eyre* are parodied in quick succession. Orlando, having been situated in London, is suddenly found 'over the moor' where, tripping and breaking her ankle, she sinks into an ecstatic reverie, murmuring

18 Thomas Dekker, 'The Great Frost. Cold doings in London, except it be at the Lottery. With News out of the Country' (1608), in *An English Garner: Ingatherings from our History and Literature*, Vol. I, ed. Edward Arber (London, 1877), pp. 84, 85. These lines are quoted, in part, by Fox.

19 From 'The Narrow Bridge of Art', in Virginia Woolf, *Granite and Rainbow* (London, 1958), p. 14.

20 Beer, *Arguing with the Past*, pp. 140, 144–6.

to herself, 'I have found my mate . . . It is the moor. I am nature's bride . . . I shall dream wild dreams. My hands shall wear no wedding ring' (p. 155). On the very next page, however, the sound of hoofbeats heralds a horseman who arrives, *à la* Rochester, in a flurry of high drama:

> she could hear the crack of a twig and the suck of the wet bog in its hoofs. The horse was almost on her. She sat upright. Towering dark against the yellow-slashed sky of dawn, with the plovers rising and falling about him, she saw a man on horseback. He started. The horse stopped.
>
> 'Madam,' the man cried, leaping to the ground, 'you're hurt!'
>
> 'I'm dead, sir!' she replied.
>
> A few minutes later, they became engaged. (p. 156)

Here, then, the romantic fiction of the Brontës, with its emphasis on transcendence through nature and fulfilment through passionate heterosexual love, is amusingly ridiculed. The 'narrowness', 'power', and 'improbability' of the Brontë world, to which Woolf referred in a critical essay,[21] are here deftly caught through parody. Nor do contemporary writers escape Woolf's satiric pen. The fictional vogue during the 1920s for 'rural fantasy and romance'[22] is comically undercut in chapter VI, as is Lawrence's literary representation of women:

> Love, the poet has said, is woman's whole existence. And if we look for a moment at Orlando writing at her table, we must admit that never was there a woman more fitted for that calling. Surely, since she is a woman, and a beautiful woman, and a woman in the prime of life, she will soon give over this pretence of writing and thinking and begin at least to think of a gamekeeper (and as long as she thinks of a man, nobody objects to a woman thinking). And then she will write him a little note (and as long as she writes little notes nobody objects to a woman writing either) and make an assignation for Sunday dusk and Sunday dusk will come; and the gamekeeper will whistle under the window – all of which is, of course, the very stuff of life and the only possible subject for fiction. (p. 168)

21 From ' "Jane Eyre" and "Wuthering Heights" ', in Virginia Woolf, *The Common Reader*, Vol. I (London, 1984), pp. 157, 160.

22 See Glen Cavaliero, *The Rural Tradition in the English Novel 1900–1939* (London, 1977), pp. x–xi.

Lawrence's *Lady Chatterley's Lover* was published in Florence during the summer of 1928. There is no biographical evidence to confirm that Virginia Woolf read Lawrence's novel during this year, although we know that she had read much of his work and found it a tedious 'display of self-conscious virility'.[23] This passage seems to suggest, however, that she had at least discussed *Lady Chatterley's Lover* with friends and wished to incorporate an ironic critique of it in her work of 1928.

Pastiche and parody, then, crystallize and evaluate certain 'view[s] of the world', metaphorically suggested by the bizarre vistas in *Orlando*. The metaphorical opposition between ice and water that runs through *Orlando* allows Woolf to develop further her case against the 'truth' of history. We are invited to contemplate how far the process of historical narrative forms itself through the freezing and preserving of certain incidents – seductive perhaps for their drama or *dramatis personae* – at the expense of other less memorable events. *Orlando*, in such a spirit of scepticism, continually draws attention to itself as a 'story' (pp. 43, 123), 'text' (p. 160), and 'narrative' (pp. 127, 180), despite its quasi-academic Preface, mock scholarly Index, and sub-title of 'A Biography'. Indeed, it deliberately foregrounds its own artifice and narrative process through metaphor. Woolf's description of the Great Frost presents it as 'a kind of petrification' (p. 22); shoals of eels, we are told, 'lay motionless in a trance' (p. 23); the bumboat woman is icily preserved and even the laughter on Orlando's lips 'froze in wonder' (p. 25). These images suggest metaphorically how the narrative of history fixes and reifies events and episodes which, in their present moment, are fleeting and evanescent; history, like the Great Frost, provides for us a window onto the past by a selective process of freezing and preserving. However, the novel, with its emphasis on inner time, is more suited than the historical study to celebrating the 'riot and confusion of the passions and emotions which every good biographer resists' (p. 11). *Orlando*, a hybrid of historical consciousness and literary imagination, charts a passage between the two. It thereby draws attention to something that obsessed Woolf throughout her writing career: the 'extraordinary discrepancy between time on the clock and time in the mind' (p. 61). Thus the Great Frost gives way to the great flood, 'a race of turbulent yellow waters', which brings about a more tangible 'riot and confusion' (p. 39). The frozen Thames breaks into great ice blocks to which 'human creatures' cling pathetically: icebergs

23 From 'An Essay in Criticism', in Virginia Woolf, *Granite and Rainbow*, p. 90.

sail away, carrying 'a table laid sumptuously for a supper of twenty; a couple in bed; together with an extraordinary number of cooking utensils' (p. 40). This image is repeated much later in the novel when the stationary traffic in London becomes 'a golden river [which] had coagulated and massed itself in golden blocks across Park Lane . . . But now, the policeman let fall his hand; the stream became liquid' (pp. 180–1). Another trip into central London sees Orlando watching

> the traffic in Oxford Street. Omnibus seemed to pile itself upon omnibus and then to jerk itself apart. So the ice blocks had pitched and tossed that day on the Thames. An old nobleman in furred slippers had sat astride one of them. There he went – she could see him now – calling down maledictions upon the Irish rebels. He had sunk there, where her car stood. (p. 190)

As well as establishing a sense of Orlando's identity across time, this metaphorical opposition between solidity and fluidity takes on an abstract meaning to do with the swirling nature of subjective time, in which the discourse of history has little place, and the more solid, reified nature of linear time, with which history deals. Similar metaphorical oppositions can be found in Woolf's other works, notably *Mrs. Dalloway* (1925), in which the constitution of the self beyond the contemporary boundaries of society is associated with images of the sea, whilst the linear time of history is represented by the hard granite of the sundial and the massive presence of Big Ben.[24] In *Orlando*, the opposition between solidity and fluidity speaks very much of the mind's relationship with historical time; of how the mind clings, as the old man clung to the iceberg, to the narrative of history amongst the 'riot and confusion' of 'the sixty or seventy different times which beat simultaneously in every normal human system' (p. 191).

Connected with this set of metaphors is that of the voyage or journey, which becomes increasingly important as *Orlando* proceeds. Woolf's interest in Elizabethan voyages, evident in the names of Drake, Hawkins, and Grenville in chapter I,[25] leads to Orlando's own voyage to Constantinople (associated here and elsewhere in Woolf's

24 For a fuller version of this argument, see Sue Zlosnik's discussion of *Mrs. Dalloway*, in Horner and Zlosnik, *Landscapes of Desire: Metaphors in Modern Women's Fiction* (Hemel Hempstead, 1990), pp. 91–114.

25 For Woolf's knowledge of Elizabethan voyages, see Fox, pp. 20–50.

work with an ambiguous sexual identity),[26] which in turn gives way to Shelmerdine's voyages around Cape Horn. These are collectively metamorphosed into the toy boat on the Serpentine which images something more abstract: 'thought, which is no more than a little toy boat' (p. 183), has taken the reader on a mental voyage through over three hundred years of a writer's life. Like history itself, however, Orlando's travels afford only a partial 'view of the world' and her later 'voyage' through London in her car expresses this insight through metaphor:

> The Old Kent Road was very crowded on Thursday, the eleventh of October 1928 . . . Here was a market. Here a funeral. Here a procession with banners upon which was written 'Ra-Un', but what else? Meat was very red. Butchers stood at the door. Women almost had their heels sliced off. Amor Vin- that was over a porch. A woman looked out of a bedroom window, profoundly contemplative and very still. Applejohn and Applebed, Undert-. Nothing could be seen whole or read from start to finish. (pp. 191–2)

Not only the past is elusive: even at a moment so precisely documented, the meaning of love, death, and the present is difficult to 'read'.

Similarly, the hero/ine's ancestral home takes on an important metaphorical dimension in *Orlando*. Associated throughout with writing and writers, the great single oak tree in its grounds is the constant inspiration for Orlando's poem. Peopled and haunted by poets and critics it is closely linked with the real Knole and Vita Sackville-West's life: the doorstopper called 'Shakespeare' at Knole no doubt provided the inspiration for the ghostly presence of the Bard throughout *Orlando*; the character of Nick Greene owes something to the Robert Greene who attacked Shakespeare, much to Edmund Gosse (as Vita recognized), and not a little to Roy Campbell, whose ingratitude for

26 In *Mrs. Dalloway*, Clarissa remembers 'failing' Richard in Constantinople (Harmondsworth, 1964; 1972), p. 36; in *To the Lighthouse*, Nancy's incipient lesbian tendencies are obliquely linked to the idea of Constantinople (Harmondsworth, 1964; 1966), p. 85. Harold Nicolson was posted to Constantinople as diplomat in 1912 and he took Vita there after their marriage in 1913; it may, therefore, have carried a coded significance for Vita, to whom *Orlando* was dedicated. A further oblique sexual allusion might also attach to both the situation of Constantinople (on the Golden Horn) and Shelmerdine's voyages round Cape Horn.

Vita's hospitality and whose cruel parody of 'The Land' earned him Woolf's contempt.[27] At the same time, however, it becomes a metaphor for the house of literary history and the woman writer's uneasy title to it. For as a Jacobean nobleman, 'afflicted with a love of literature' (p. 46), Orlando is confident, well educated in the classics, and prolific: 'he had written, before he was turned twenty-five, some forty-seven plays, histories, romances, poems', despite the fact that 'to publish, was, he knew, for a nobleman an inexpiable disgrace' (p. 48). Although his own work does not bring him any literary acclaim, he becomes a patron of the arts and promises to pay Nick Greene a pension throughout his life. Orlando's experience as a woman writer is very different. Soon after her metamorphosis, hampered by lack of writing materials, she expresses great frustration – 'Oh! if only I could write!' she cries – and thenceforth confines her work to 'a few margins and blank spaces in the manuscript of "The Oak Tree" ' (p. 91). In the sparkling society of Queen Anne's England she hides her manuscripts away when interrupted (p. 116), although privately she is 'apt to think of poetry when she should [be] thinking of taffeta' (p. 121). Reduced to pouring out tea for Pope, Swift, and Addison (whose works are exposed as decidedly misogynistic), she is nevertheless influenced by their style, 'so that . . . she [writes] some very pleasant, witty verses and characters in prose' (p. 132). However, internalizing their condescension, she comes to see herself as fortunate muse rather than creative artist: 'she lavished her wine on them and put bank-notes, which they took very kindly, beneath their plates at dinner, and accepted their dedications, and thought herself highly honoured by the exchange' (p. 132). To escape the extreme gender polarization of this period, Orlando occasionally disguises herself as a man. For her literary reputation, however, this is a disaster: 'she often occurs in contemporary memoirs as 'Lord' So-and-so, who was in fact her cousin; her bounty is ascribed to him, and it is he who is said to have written the poems that were really hers' (p. 137). In Victorian England, the 'spirit of the age' takes Orlando and breaks her (p. 152), so that she comes to

27 See, respectively, Schlack, *Continuing Presences*, pp. 85–7; Glendinning, *Vita*, pp. 202 (for Gosse), 175–6, 179–80, 182–4, 239 (for Campbell). Although Roy Campbell's *The Georgiad*, a parody of Sackville-West's 'The Land' and a fierce attack on Bloomsbury, the Georgian poets, and the Nicolsons, was not published until 1931, Glendinning asserts that Vita saw the poem 'well in advance of its publication' (p. 239). It is likely, then, that Woolf would also have seen *The Georgiad* or been told of its content by Vita.

crave marriage and someone upon whom she can 'lean' (p. 153). The asphyxiating atmosphere of this period with its emphasis on marriage and procreation recalls Woolf's complaint in *Moments of Being* that

> Society in those days was a very competent machine. It was convinced that girls must be changed into married women. It had no doubts, no mercy; no understanding of any other wish; of any other gift. Nothing was taken seriously.[28]

The result for Orlando's literary output is, again, disastrous: 'Her page was written in the neatest sloping Italian hand with the most insipid verse she had ever read in her life' (p. 149). Only the present fully restores the happiness of writing to Orlando, since only the Elizabethan period and the twentieth century allow her to exercise her androgynous nature, the mark, according to Woolf in *A Room of One's Own*, of a 'great mind'.[29] It is fitting, then, that *Orlando* closes with the hero/ine returning to the family home of Knole, which, with its 365 bedrooms (p. 67) and its 52 staircases (p. 70), comes to represent the temporal house of literary history. It is a house which has been previously leased and possessed by the male literary establishment; one to which the woman writer has had only tenuous title and from which she has been dispossessed historically – a fact reflected in Orlando's long legal battle for her home. Described several times in *Orlando* as more like a town than a house (pp. 12, 66, 105) and built by 'workmen whose names are unknown' (p. 66), Knole metamorphoses from an 'anonymous work of creation' (p. 66) owned by the aristocracy into a spectral great house – 'all its windows robed in silver. Of wall or substance there was none' (p. 205) – which Orlando no longer sees as her own, but which belongs 'to time now: to history: . . . past the touch and control of the living' (p. 199). Here the alternative literary history of *Orlando* is presented as 'miasma' or 'mirage'; it is given a ghostly palimpsestic presence which challenges the solid authority of all that Knole metaphorically represents. It is thus not surprising to find that writing *Orlando* led Woolf to consider further projects which would offer alternative histories for women:

28 Virginia Woolf, *Moments of Being* (London, 1978; 1986), p. 157.
29 Virginia Woolf, *A Room of One's Own* (Hardmondsworth 1945; 1972), p. 97.

> Well but Orlando was the outcome of a perfectly definite, indeed overmastering impulse. I want fun. I want fantasy. I want (& this was serious) to give things their caricature value. And still this mood hangs about me. I want to write a history, say of Newnham or the womans *[sic]* movement, in the same vein. (*Diary*, III. 203)

The search for a 'true' historical text, or one authoritative 'view of the world', is, then, something of a wild goose chase, a fact Woolf's woman historian comes to recognize intuitively in 'The Journal of Miss Joan Martyn': 'I had been on some expedition, a wild goose chase it was, to recover some documents which I believed to lie buried in the ruins of Caister Abbey' (*The Complete Shorter Fiction*, p. 51). In similar spirit, the last section of *Orlando* is marked by the swooping presence of birds – that of jay, kingfisher, hawk, thrush, starling, and wild goose. Associated with the flights of fancy which dominate *Orlando*, birds are emblematic of the human imagination and its tendency to soar above the 'facts' of life; they are a reminder that history represents no absolute truth and that, since its embodiment is textual, it is always susceptible to invention, revision, and the competing presence of literature as historical record.

Like Orlando, we are made urgently aware of 'the pressure of the present' (p.201) at the end of the book; here, linear narrative, to which the past so easily succumbs, gradually disintegrates and gives way to the unscripted present with its 'nondescript character' (p. 201). Orlando's story dissolves into a series of epiphanies which spring from 'the dark pool of the mind' (p. 204). The strident striking of clocks throughout the last section culminates in a closure which brings together 'time on the clock', recorded faithfully in date and moment (the book's actual date of publication), and the wilder 'time in the mind' that frees the individual from historical determinism and linear progression:

> And as Shelmerdine, now grown a fine sea captain, hale, fresh-coloured, and alert, leapt to the ground, there sprang up over his head a single wild bird.
>
> 'It is the goose!' Orlando cried. 'The wild goose . . .'
>
> And the twelfth stroke of midnight sounded; the twelfth stroke of midnight, Thursday, the eleventh of October, Nineteen Hundred and Twenty Eight. (p. 205)

In writing *Orlando*, Virginia Woolf set out to amuse herself, express her love for Vita Sackville-West, and, as Harold Nicolson observed, restore Knole to Vita for ever, thus defying the dictates of history.[30] *Orlando* also gives us, however, a disquisition on the relationship between literature and history in which the authority of the latter is undermined satirically by the former. It makes plain the 'difficult business' of historical 'time-keeping' and proves that 'nothing more quickly disorders it than contact with any of the arts' (p. 191).

30 Harold Nicolson wrote to Vita in 1928 that *Orlando* was 'a book in which you and Knole are identified for ever, a book which will perpetuate that identity into years when both you and I are dead' (Glendinning, p. 205).

Cousin Bette: *Balzac and the Historiography of Difference*

SCOTT McCRACKEN

In recent years post-structuralism has challenged a historically-based criticism. Post-structuralist critics have emphasised textuality and 'difference' where historical critics have used contextual analysis or historical interpretation. Fredric Jameson has described textuality as

> a methodological hypothesis whereby the objects of study of the human sciences . . . are considered to constitute so many texts that we *decipher* and *interpret*, as distinguished from the older views of those realities and existants or substances that we in one way or another attempt to *know*.[1]

This approach has been valuable in that it has often opened up totalising or one-sided interpretations to more complex, open, and pluralist readings. A disadvantage has been that the refusal of any one interpretation has sometimes meant that, for post-structuralists, history is just a series of texts with no necessary explanatory value. At the same time, books like Hayden White's *Metahistory* and Fredric Jameson's *The Political Unconscious* have argued the importance of a narrative form in historical criticism.

Balzac criticism has exemplified these debates, from Lukács's classic Marxist account of a general historical approach to the novel in *Studies in European Realism* to Barthes's minutely detailed 'plural commentary' on Balzac's novella *Sarrasine* in *S/Z*. Both critics have been subjected to a rigorous critique by Fredric Jameson, Lukács in *The Political Unconscious*, and Barthes in Jameson's recently updated essay, 'The Ideology of the Text'. My own essay gives an outline of the debate between the three critics and suggests some ways in

1 Fredric Jameson, 'The Ideology of the Text', in *The Ideologies of Theory: Essays 1971–1986*, 2 vols (London, 1988), I. 18.

which it might be possible to posit a relationship between the narrative structure of Balzac's *Cousin Bette* and 'difference' as it manifests itself in the text.

If history is about dates then *Cousin Bette* is self-evidently an historical novel. The narrative is structured around a specific set of dates and these act as important signifiers in the text. From the opening sentence, 'Towards the middle of July in the year 1838', to the events in the penultimate paragraph, 'on 1 February 1846', we are invited to associate actions and time in order to produce a meaningful narrative. Characters date themselves. Crevel's bodily movements, 'by their undisguised heaviness, are as indiscreet as a birth certificate'. The first scene takes place in a room which is dated in two senses. It is both in a state of disrepair and out of fashion:

> The Baroness sat down on a little sofa that must certainly have been very pretty about the year 1809, and motioned Crevel to an armchair decorated with bronzed sphinx heads, from which the paint was scaling off, leaving the bare wood exposed in places.[2]

These descriptive details place the two characters, Crevel and Baroness Hulot, in a historically delimited space, to which each has a different relationship. For Adeline Hulot, the furnishings, from the imperial, Napoleonic period, represent her past, youth, and faded beauty. For Crevel, the room, the historical period it represents, and Adeline herself are all objects to be conquered, or, in the more prosaic terms of the 1830s, to be bought. In *The Age of Revolution* Eric Hobsbawn writes that the 'revolutionary wave of 1830 . . . marks the definitive defeat of aristocratic by bourgeois power in Western Europe'. Crevel presents himself with the irony of the ascendant power: 'I am a tradesman, a shopkeeper, a former retailer of almond paste, eau-de-Portugal, cephalic oil for hair troubles' (p. 16).

This relationship between the character, time, and space, Engels called 'the truthful reproduction of typical characters under typical

2 Honoré de Balzac, *Cousin Bette*, trans. Marion Ayton Crawford, Penguin Classics (Harmondsworth, 1965; 1981), p. 14 (hereafter by page reference in text).

circumstances',[3] opposing it to late nineteenth-century naturalism; and it is Lukács, following Engels, who has done most to develop the idea of typicality in twentieth-century criticism. Characters represent a nexus of contradictory social forces within Lukács's Marxist historiography:

> The Marxist philosophy of history is a comprehensive doctrine dealing with the necessary progress made by humanity from primitive communism to our own time and the perspectives of our further advance along the same road [;] as such it also gives us indications for the historical future. But such indications – born of the recognition of certain laws governing historical development – are not a cookery book providing recipes for each phenomenon or period . . . but a signpost pointing the direction in which history moves forward.[4]

In so far as this is an evolutionary view of history, it is Hegelian rather than Darwinian (harking back to Lukács's earlier work, published in 1923, *The Theory of the Novel*). The typical is a contradictory category related to a socio-historical totality which the realist novel can only attempt to represent. Lukács follows Engels by putting this in terms of a relationship between Balzac's personal political stance and the representation of history in his novels. According to Engels this was itself contradictory:

> Balzac was politically a Legitimist; his great work is a constant elegy on the irretrievable decay of good society; his sympathies are all with the class doomed to extinction. But for all that his satyre [*sic*] is never keener, his irony never bitterer than when he sets in motion the very men and women with whom he sympathises most deeply – the nobles. And the only men of whom he always speaks with undisguised admiration, are his bitterest political antagonists, the republican heroes of the Cloître Saint Merri [Méry], the men who at that time (1830–36) were indeed the representatives of the popular masses.[5]

3 Frederick Engels to Margaret Harkness, April 1898, in *Marx and Engels on Literature and Art*, ed. Stefan Morawiski (New York, 1973), p. 115.
4 Georg Lukács, *Studies in European Realism*, introduction by Alfred Kazin (New York, 1964), pp. 3–4 (essays first published 1935–39).
5 *Marx and Engels on Literature and Art*, p. 116.

Lukács agrees that Balzac, himself representative of the historical contradictions of the time, tries to 'present a totality' in his series of novels, *La Comédie Humaine*.

Typicality has to represent not the average, which is Lukács's criticism of Zola's naturalism, but rather

> Balzac builds his plots on broader foundations than any other author before or after him, but nevertheless there is nothing in them not germane to the story. The many sided influence of multifariously determined factors in them is in perfect conformity with the structure of objective reality whose wealth we can never adequately grasp and reflect with our all too abstract, all too rigid, all too direct, all too unilateral thinking.[6]

Lukács's concept of realism has subsequently come under heavy attack from post-structuralists, particularly the idea that there could be 'perfect conformity' between the plot (despite the 'multifariously determined factors') and 'objective reality'. Yet, there appears to be a level on which *Cousin Bette* works in the way Lukács describes. The plot represents typical aspects of the eight year period covered by the novel, 1838–46 (the novel was itself published in 1846); and as such it is typical of the economic and political changes under the Orléanist regime. The novel centres upon a typical family established in the Napoleonic period, an origin which is sufficiently dubious to provide what Lukács calls 'for Balzac the central problem of French social history'. The family wealth has been accrued through the Baron's position as Commissary general, and his wife's family owes its money to foraging contracts during the Napoleonic wars. While no aristocratic families dating back to before 1789 appear in the novel, and the representative of the republicanism of '89, Marshal Hulot, is a member of the establishment, not a leader of the 'popular masses', the lack of an established ruling class betrays a crisis of legitimacy, and society is perceived to be unstable.

The seeds of Hulot's downfall have been sown long before the novel opens, but it is his inability to compete with the wily financier Crevel which dramatises his decline. Crevel's skills are more suited to the economic climate of the 1830s and 1840s and less to the

6 Lukács, p. 58.

heroic period prior to 1815 to which Hector so obviously belongs. Hector's desperate attempt to escape from financial ruin is only a futile attempt to re-enact his earlier career, which transferred to the new terrain of Algeria exposes the family to the scandal of corruption. The family's salvation and return to political grace come *via* the heroic Hector's son, also aptly named, Victorin. Victorin, as attorney and parliamentarian, represents the new, considerably less charismatic hero of the age. He is able to negotiate the new state structures in order to extricate the family from the grip of his father's mistress, Mme Marneffe, and her accomplice, Cousin Bette.

Hayden White has analysed the narrative tropes of nineteenth-century historiography as the metaphoric, the metonymic, the synecdochic, and the ironic, corresponding to romance, tragedy, comedy, and satire respectively.[7] The metonymic clash between old Napoleonic and new commercial values in *Cousin Bette* makes Hector's tragedy the dominant narrative trope of the novel. The Baron's downfall acts as a representative example of the dashing of an aristocratic ideal in the 1830s; although the illegitimate origin of his title betrays the gap between that ideal and any real possibilities of a return to before 1789. There is a sense of textual play which suggests that rather than nostalgically looking to the past, the novel experiments with the configurations of history on offer. Deprived of a military arena Hulot turns to a 'campaign on women', which, as he gives it the same energy he once gave to war, assumes an unreal, theatrical quality. In the final stages of his defeat he is helped to disappear by one of his former mistresses, an opera singer, whom he has helped onto the stage and who now admires the operatic quality of his demise:

> 'I'd rather have a proper spendthrift, mad about women, like you, than one of those cold soul-less bankers who are supposed to be so virtuous and ruin thousands of families with their golden railways . . . You have only ruined your own family; the only property you've sold is you!' (p. 341)

7 Hayden White, *Metahistory: The Historical Imagination in Nineteenth Century Europe* (Baltimore, 1973), pp. 31–8.

This dramatic or theatrical element in Balzac's fiction suggests a degree of reflexivity in the text which is not allowed for by Lukács.

Balzac employs a method of dramatic confrontation which is neatly exemplified in the first scene between Adeline and Crevel. The historically delimited space of the drawing room becomes a stage, which the Baroness prepares before the dialogue can take place. As if to underline the fragile and temporary nature of that space we learn, through Adeline's scene-setting, of at least four potential avenues of disruption:

> Only a thin partition divided this room from the boudoir, whose window opened on the garden, and Madame Hulot left Monsieur Crevel alone for a moment, considering it necessary to shut both the window and the boudoir door so that no one could eavesdrop on that side. She even took the precaution of closing the french window of the drawing-room, smiling as she did so at her daughter and cousin, whom she saw installed in an old summer-house at the far end of the garden. Returning, she left the door of the card-room ajar, so that she might hear the drawing-room door open if anyone should come in. (pp. 13–14)

Adeline's actions develop a number of dramatic possibilities within the scene, helping to relate her dialogue with Crevel to possible actions. The french window holds in stasis the plot lines embodied in Hortense and Lisbeth. In the ensuing discussion Crevel makes declarations of love with menaces to Adeline; one of his threats is that he will not provide any money for Hortense's dowry. The door of the card-room signals the possible entrance of Adeline's husband, while Crevel uses his knowledge of Hector's infidelities in an attempt to break down her resistance.

The scene seems to work because of the artificiality of its dramatic setting rather than through its relationship to any historical truth. The reader's attention is drawn towards the temporal and spatial limits of the representation given. Within the crucible of those limits the 'typical' situation contains the possibility of bursting out of its fragile boundaries and mutating into a new situation. It is only within this context of a provisional conceptualisation of an historical moment, that it is possible to accept the more extreme and melodramatic actions of Balzac's characters, which otherwise would appear to destroy any consensus about the text's realism.

Such a moment occurs when the Hulot children throw themselves at the feet of their father, because he has returned (as it transpires only temporarily) to the domestic hearth. This passionate moment of familial harmony has to be interrupted to prevent an embarrassing closure which would prevent the dramatic action from progressing. The temporary nature of the reconciliation is confirmed by the unexpected entrance of the Marshal Hulot, shattering the moment: 'The two young people rose, and they all made an effort to cover their emotion' (p. 270).

The dramatic nature of Balzac's realism and the episodic nature of the narrative raises two related problems with Lukács's historical criticism. The textual play which is an integral part of Balzac's writing does not submit easily even to a 'many-sided reality' and this in turn must complicate Lukács's relationship between the text and a totalising historiography.

Barthes's project in *S/Z* is to decouple the relationship between narrative and totality:

> inventory, explanation, and digression may deter any observation of suspense, may even separate verb and complement, noun and attribute; the work of the commentary, once it is separated from any ideology of totality, consists precisely in *manhandling* the text, *interrupting* it. What is thereby denied is not the quality of the text (here incomparable) but its 'naturalness'.[8]

On this final point there is some agreement between Lukács and Barthes. Both object to 'naturalness' as a category which denies the act of representation. Where they differ is on the relationship of the text to a 'real' history. Barthes uses 'textuality' to show the text as source of a multiplicity of meanings rather than the narrative's relationship to totality, which must be a reduction of plurality. For Barthes,

> rereading draws the text out of its internal chronology ('this happens *before* or *after* that') and recaptures a mythic time (without *before* or *after*) . . . (. . . there is no *first* reading, even if the text is concerned to give us that illusion by several operations of

[8] Roland Barthes, *S/Z*, trans. Richard Miller (London, 1975), p. 15 (first published Paris, 1970).

> *suspense*, artifices more spectacular than persuasive); rereading is no longer consumption, but play (that play which is the return of the different).[9]

Now, immersed in the world of criticism post-Barthes, it is impossible not to see the attractions of this approach. In fact, it is easier now to think 'naturally' along Barthesian lines than along Lukácsian. We accept that there is no first reading, that the text can be broken down (*brisé*) into a plurality of socially constructed codes, codes we already know, which we have already read. Lukács, in comparison, appears crude, irrevocably wedded to a formal conception of historical progress. The disadvantage of Barthes's commentary is that if we accept the concept of 'mythic time', the problem of the relationship between text and history is solved by abolishing history altogether.

To subject *Cousin Bette* to a post-structuralist, plural commentary is to allow aspects of the text to be foregrounded which are subordinated or marginalised by Lukács's historical criticism. Adeline's desire to shut out her husband and her daughter can be read as both a dramatic device and as a textual strategy. Just as Adeline is described as 'suffering as a woman, a mother and a wife', and is thus defined by three codes of socialised femininity, so Hortense's unmarried state is part of a discourse of feminine sexuality. Hortense's position in the garden with Bette could be read as virginal innocence with Bette as predatory serpent, – Adeline's shutting the french window would then be a futile attempt to protect her. In this reading, sexual desire is a present but unknown force to Hortense, but to Adeline and Crevel, engaged in negotiating her future, its social significance is clear:

> '. . . There are days when she wanders sadly in the garden, not knowing why. I find her with tears in her eyes.'
>
> 'She is twenty-one,' said Crevel. (p. 27)

Another reading might see Hortense as having already lost her innocence as it is Hortense who appears to desire Bette's lover (and, in fact, she later marries him). Hortense's majority creates a social

9 Barthes, p. 16.

crisis which cannot be contained or fully understood in terms of what I have described as the dominant narrative trope of the novel: the metonymic clash of values between Hector and Crevel.

> 'Ought I to send her to a convent?' said the Baroness. 'At such times of crisis religion is often powerless against nature, and the most piously brought up girls lose their heads!' (p. 27)

Hortense's femininity is an unstable element within the text, and as such it allows a deconstruction of the social codes which would define a feminine sexuality as other. Hortense's desire, between girlhood and matrimony, represents an aporia in the narrative structure. Barthes's method of breaking down the text permits us to unknot the codes which cannot explain that desire in their own terms. In contrast, Valérie Marneffe's sexual drive is at one with her drive for wealth, status, and power. This process of decoding does, however, reveal the dominant narrative trope as gendered: Hulot's tragedy is the tragedy of a type of heroic masculinity as much as that of a class created by the Napoleonic period. A plural commentary, as advocated by Barthes, draws out what Derrida calls *différence* in the text, and in Derridean terms this should deconstruct the metaphysic of presence; but, as we have seen, the novel already presents us with a society in which nothing seems certain, further complicating Lukács's attempt to insert history as an explanatory term.

It should be noted, however, that despite the fact that the relationship between text and history is complicated in a plural commentary, it is not absent. There is still an underlying assumption of an historical narrative. Fredric Jameson argues that

> all apparently synchronic or ahistorical analysis depends on and presupposes (for the most part covertly) a diachronic scheme, a vision or 'philosophy' of history, a historical 'master-narrative,' in terms of which its evaluations are processed.[10]

Strictly speaking, to describe Hortense as having an individual sexuality is an anachronism in the 1830s, since the idea of having an identity which is defined by sexual desire belongs to the late nine-

10 Fredric Jameson, 'The Ideology of the Text', I. 54–5.

teenth-century. While Balzac's text does not endow Hortense with an identity defined by her desires, part of the decoding process involves using a more recent concept in order to understand the text as historical. It is, in effect, employing an historical master narrative, here, a history of the subject in relation to desire.

The other category of difference which post-structuralist thought has helped to disentangle from the grand narratives which would seek to marginalise it, is that of race. Balzac's pedagogic statements about his characters include significant judgements on the basis of racial or national characteristics. In his representation of Steinbock, the aristocratic Polish artist, Balzac's sense of a French national identity is quite distinct. It places France at the centre of a European civilisation, from which Poland is excluded:

> All Slavs have a childish side, as have all primitive races that have rather made incursion among civilised nations than become properly civilised themselves. (p. 229)

Coming from an even more peripheral quarter (in relation to France), and hence acting as a more powerful source of instability within the text, is Baron Henri Montès de Montejanos, the Brazilian lover of Valérie Marneffe, who returns from his isolated plantation to reclaim her. The Baron's psychology is described in terms of his environmental and racial background:

> Monsieur le Baron Henri Montès de Montejanos, the product of an equatorial climate, had the physique and complexion that we all associate with Othello. (p. 181)

Montejanos is an example of how the text is pluralised by racial difference, but as a character he also has an important role in the resolution of the plot.

While Jameson has criticised Lukács's too ready assumption that Balzac's 'sense of historical realities inflects his [Lukács's] own personal wishes in the direction of social and historical versimilitude',[11] in his essay, 'The Ideology of the Text', he argues that content must not be ignored. In his own account of *Sarrasine*, Jameson argues that

11 Fredric Jameson, *The Political Unconscious* (London, 1981), p. 164.

Balzac's use of the novella – a literary form which originated in the renaissance – demonstrates a logic of content which Barthes cannot escape:

> Barthes' 'hermeneutic code' can now at any rate be seen to be either excessively or insufficiently theorized, insofar as its specific object of study or raw material (what happened? when will we learn what happened?) is a historical form, the art-novella, on the point of artificial revival, and also extinction.[12]

The logic of content of *Cousin Bette* can be described as the relationship between the dramatic scenes described above and the narrative organisation of tragedy. In *Cousin Bette* it is Shakespearian tragedy rather than the art-novella, which structures the narrative. Within Balzac's nineteenth-century novel Shakespeare's tragedies provide a model for a progressive history of the subject in relation to socio-historical change; but the structural limitations of this model are clear.

Baron Hulot's heroic, masculine, and French identity disintegrates on impact with the market values embodied by Crevel, but his son, Victorin, displays an increasing authority in the new political and economic climate. In order to rescue the family's fortunes, Victorin uses the relationship between the legal apparatus of the state and its obverse, the Parisian criminal underworld, to destroy the now married Valérie and Crevel – in that order, thus saving his wife's inheritance. The organisation which mediates between the underworld and families like the Hulots is the police. Although they refuse to intervene directly (we learn that they used to, but this is no longer the policy) they put Victorin in touch with the shadowy Mme Nourisson. She, while representative of criminality rather than the police (legality and illegality often blur in *La Comédie Humaine*, most famously in the figure of Vautrin, criminal turned chief of police), is also an agent rather than an actor. Her skill is in using Montejanos's jealousy to get him to murder the newly-weds.

The murder itself is performed in a manner which marks it as the work of a 'primitive' and 'untamed' sexuality, for Montejanos is 'one of the children of nature'. The method is an obscure tropical poison

12 'The Ideology of the Text', I. 53.

which cannot be diagnosed and the antidote for which exists only in Brazil. This otherness, which is composed of a plurality of bourgeois fears and the anxieties of class, race, and sexuality, is utilised by Victorin to limit the damage that can be done to future middle-class security by the out-of-control patriarchs of the previous generation, Crevel and Hector. Hector's tragedy is defused, and is itself marginalised because Victorin is able to employ those aspects of social otherness which that narrative trope cannot explain.

This account of the relationship of the narrative structure of the novel to historical change is preferable to the post-structuralist account of a new linguistic freedom under capitalism, which seems to rely on general statements about changes in the mode of production:

> The difference between feudal society and bourgeois society, index and sign, is this: the index has an origin, the sign does not: to shift from index to sign is to abolish the last (or first) limit, the origin, the basis, the prop, to enter into the limitless process of equivalences, representations that nothing will ever stop, orient, fix, sanction.[13]

If the limits of this new freedom are not defined, then the valid wish to escape the metaphysic of presence can create more problems than it solves by employing the concept of the free-floating signifier and 'mythic time'. The antipathy of post-structuralist criticism to theories of narrative is demonstrated by Foucault's use of *Don Quixote* to prove the same point that Barthes makes about *Sarrasine*:

> *Don Quixote* is a negative of the Renaissance world; writing has ceased to be the prose of the world; resemblances and signs have dissolved their former alliance; similitudes have become deceptive and verge upon the visionary or madness; things still remain stubbornly within their ironic identity: they are no longer anything but what they are; words wander off on their own . . .[14]

13 Barthes, p. 40.
14 Michel Foucault, *The Order of Things* (London, 1970), pp. 47–8 (first published Paris, 1966).

If it is possible to say the same thing about Cervantes's novel as it is about those of Balzac, written two hundred years later, then it appears that periodisation, which must be one of the tools of the historical criticism, has been rejected out of hand by post-structuralism.

This argument brings us back to Lukács, who notes Balzac's use of older literary forms, but Jameson's argument with Lukács is that he

> is right about Balzac, but for the wrong reasons: not Balzac's deeper sense of political and historical realities, but rather his incorrigible fantasy demands ultimately raise History itself over against him, as absent cause, as that on which desire must come to grief.[15]

Jameson would then replace Lukács's use of typicality with an interpretation of Balzac's characters as allegorical. This is his approach in his early essay on *Cousin Bette*, but while this methodology acts as a way of historicising a post-structuralist, linguistically-based commentary, its heavy use of Freudian psychoanalysis in unearthing the text's 'political unconscious' is of limited use when it comes to an analysis of sexual and racial difference. In this allegorical system, he places Bette in the position of super-ego; Hulot as the id; and Mme Hulot as the ego, 'the place of the *subject*, the rational consciousness that is the battleground between these two buffeting forces'.[16] While this Freudian system is historicised as part of a narrative of class, Jameson is unable to account for what he sees as the apparently motiveless malevolence of Balzac's women characters, particularly as represented by the character of Cousin Bette herself. Jameson's own account of Lisbeth uses a rather crude, pre-feminist 'psychology of the old maid': her character is 'distorted by repression.'[17]

This must be an inadequate account of the eponymous Bette and of the role of characters like Montejanos. The role of Montejanos as both destabilising, pluralising element and as narrative device demonstrates that it is possible to provide an account of the relationship between narrative structure and the text as *écriture*. An interpreta-

15 *The Political Unconscious*, p. 183.

16 Fredric Jameson, '*La Cousine Bette* and Allegorical Realism', *PMLA*, 86 (1971), 253.

17 '*La Cousine Bette* and Allegorical Realism', p. 248.

tion of, rather than a plural commentary on, the representations of race within the text would have to draw attention to the other use of a racial other within the narrative structure, that is, Hulot's attempt to rescue his fortunes through foraging contracts in Algeria. The events which make up this sub-plot of imperial adventurism are only represented in terms of their effects on the Parisian centre. Hulot fails to bring off the scheme because the techniques of accumulation which worked so well before 1815 are not applicable to the new conditions of North Africa. As with Victorin's success in manipulating the power of the state, there is a relationship between the construction of the subject and the narrative structure. The historical account of Algerian imperialism is related to Hulot's degeneration, not only physically (he appears to age ten years), but also as a viable and coherent centre within the text. This is not to say that the text does not reveal itself as plural, but that the extent of meaning which can be read off depends on an historical approach which reads Balzac not as 'unrelated diversity' (this is Jameson's term for Barthes's rereading) but as a diversity which is related to a narrative structure, implying an historiography. The categories which post-structuralism has helped us to read into literary texts, of race, gender, and sexuality, might then be seen as having their own histories, as categories which become important in textual analysis because of the social movements which have used them as their banners.

If we look at Bette in the same way she appears as both central character and – representative of the drive to ruin the Hulot family – as the most important source of textual incoherence. Her removal from the scene, thanks to a timely chest infection, is an essential pre-requisite for the novelistic closure. Bette is a traditional novelistic device. Her lack of definite social position as poor relation, servant, old maid, allows her to move from stage to stage, while other characters are caught in and defined by the delimited spatial and temporal zones described above. She is a line of communication between Valérie – whose position as bourgeois prostitute is similarly transgressive – and Crevel, as well as between the Hulot family and more peripheral characters such as Steinbock and Montejanos.

Far from being an agent of repression, within the structure of the novel, Bette works as a pluralising device in opposition to the unilateral history of the subject provided by Hulot's tragedy. With an understanding of Bette's role we can see that Balzac's use of Shakespearian tragedy is also plural, incorporating Lear – the tragedy of the family; Antony – the dissolution of heroism into sensuality; and Othello – the tragedy of sexual jealousy and the murder of the object of desire.

The epic-drama of Balzacian narrative means that the social codes of Barthes's plural commentary can be read off more easily than in a naturalist or modernist text. Balzac's realism allows characters to stand out against the narrative structure. There is no easy relationship here between the construction of the subject and narrative, with the result that Balzac's attempted naturalisation of sexual or racial difference is easily denaturalised by the modern reader or historical critic. Bette's 'primitive' nature or Steinbock's 'childishness' are not fully reified into an ideology of racial or sexual inferiority. Reading now, consciously or unconsciously, we read through and against late nineteenth-century naturalism with its scientific categories of race and gender and through and against modernist *écriture*, where ideologies of difference are subsumed, for example in Conrad, into reified subjectivities.

Any historical approach to literature must be inadequate if it cannot account for sexual and racial difference. In *The Political Unconscious* Jameson proceeds too quickly through his own interpretative model to a history of metasynchronous modes of production, bypassing the interrelated complexity of gender, race, class, and sexuality in the history of the subject.[18] There are occasional hints dropped in *The Political Unconscious*, suggesting, for example, a theory of sexuality which sees Freud's project as part of a more general autonomisation of the senses; but while Jameson leaves us with valuable methodological clues, he does not follow them up himself.

A methodology which works better at the micro-level of the history of the subject is Peter Dews's Adornian critique of Derridean post-structuralism. Adorno argues for a history of the subject which recognizes that 'identity thinking' is part of an act of self-preservation in which the 'contingency and difference of nature leaves scars'.[19] Consciousness is unfolded in 'concrete experience', experi-

18 *The Political Unconscious*, ch. 1, especially pp. 74–102.
19 Peter Dews, *The Logics of Disintegration* (London, 1988), p. 39.

ence which is part of a socio-historical development. As a text, *Cousin Bette* allows several approaches to an historical understanding, including Lukács's argument for a totality that is directly apprehendable from the text and which conforms to a history of concrete experience; but, while Balzac's realism does allow a neat historical reading, the history of the subject which is made prominent by Baron Hulot's tragedy bears a complex relationship with the novelistic structure. A post-naturalist, post-modernist interpretation would need to draw back from the coherence of Hulot's history and to contemplate the incoherence of Hortense or Montejanos. This need not be a post-modernist celebration of heterogeneity in the name of difference, rather it would be to recognise that the text's own master narrative of tragedy functions in relation to the formal representation of difference in Balzac's dramatic scenes. These scenes construct provisional, discontinuous identities within the text, fixing the construction of the subject in time and space. Lukács is right to see the clash of values which that tragedy exemplifies as the explanatory master narrative of Balzac's fiction, but the provisional nature of Balzac's historical, dramatic moments makes dangerous any attempt to relate them back to even a contradictory historical unity. Accepting that these moments are what Adorno calls non-concepts is not the same thing as saying an objective history does not exist, but that

> history is *not* a text, not a narrative, master or otherwise, but that as an abstract cause, it is inaccessible to us except in textual form, and that our approach to it, and to the Real itself, necessarily passes through its prior textualisation, its narrativisation in the political unconscious.[20]

In philosophical terms, these moments are non-concepts within which a non-identity persists as a necessary illusion, a pre-condition of meaning: 'In truth all concepts, even the philosophical ones, refer to nonconceptualities, because concepts on their part are moments of the reality that requires their formation'.[21] They need to be read historically, that is as non-concepts which are part of Balzac's own

20 *The Political Unconscious*, p. 35.

21 Theodore Adorno, *Negative Dialectics*, trans. E. B. Ashton (London, 1973), p. 11 (first published Frankfurt am Main, 1966).

nineteenth-century historiography and now as non-concepts which we read through subsequent literary texts as well as through the non-concepts of gender and race which have 'complicated' history as a result of, for example, anti-imperialist struggles and the women's movement. This 'complication' requires a more complex though also much richer historiography, an historiography of difference.

Notes on editor and contributors

Angus Easson is Professor of English and Chairman of the Modern Languages Department at Salford University. He has published widely on nineteenth-century literature and edited works by Dickens and Elizabeth Gaskell. His study of Elizabeth Gaskell appeared in 1979 and *Elizabeth Gaskell: The Critical Heritage* in 1991. He is joint editor of vol. 7 of the Pilgrim Edition of Dickens's letters.

Andrew Gibson is Senior Lecturer in English at Royal Holloway and Bedford New College, University of London. He is the author of *Reading Narrative Discourse* (1990) and has published widely on modern literature. He founded and organizes the London University Seminar for research on Joyce's *Ulysses*. He is currently working on a study of *Ulysses* and a volume of essays on Pound. He also writes fiction for children.

Avril Horner is Lecturer in English in the Modern Languages Department at Salford University. She teaches Virginia Woolf on the University's Master's degree. She has published on the poetry of Geoffrey Hill and, with Sue Zlosnik, is author of *Landscapes of Desire: Metaphors in Modern Women's Fiction* (1990).

Claire Lamont is Head of English Literature in the School of English at the University of Newcastle upon Tyne. Her research interests are in Johnson, Austen, and Scott, and in oral literature. She is currently editing Scott's *Chronicles of the Canongate* for the Edinburgh Edition of the Waverley Novels and is working on the publication of Scott's novels in America.

Scott McCracken is Lecturer in English in the Modern Languages Department of Salford University. He is currently completing his thesis, on gender and narrative structure in English writing 1880–1920. He is editing a volume of essays entitled *People's History and Popular Culture* and is a member of the editorial collective of *Red Letters*.

Leonee Ormond is Reader in English at King's College, University of London. She has published books on George du Maurier, Lord Leighton (with Richard Ormond), and J. M. Barrie, and numerous articles on nineteenth- and twentieth-century literature, nineteenth-century art, and connections between literature and painting. She is completing a 'contextual' biography of Tennyson.

Terence Wright is Lecturer in English Literature in the School of English at the University of Newcastle upon Tyne. He has published widely on theoretical aspects of the novel and produced a study of *Tess of the D'Urbervilles*. He is currently working on fiction and the sense of transcendence.

DATE DUE

JUN 30 1996

GAYLORD PRINTED IN U.S.A.